A Grayscale Coloring Book

by Julia Spiri

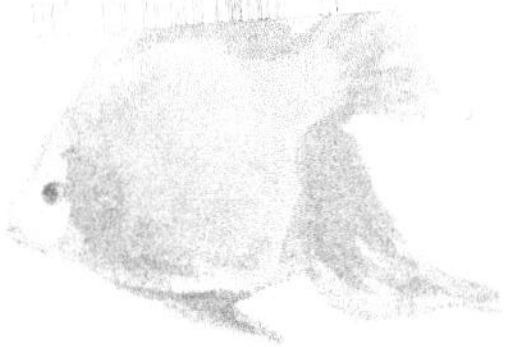

The Inspiration

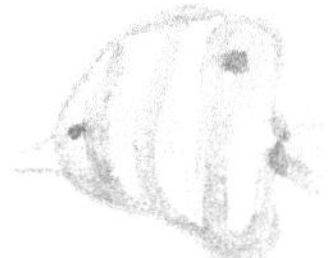

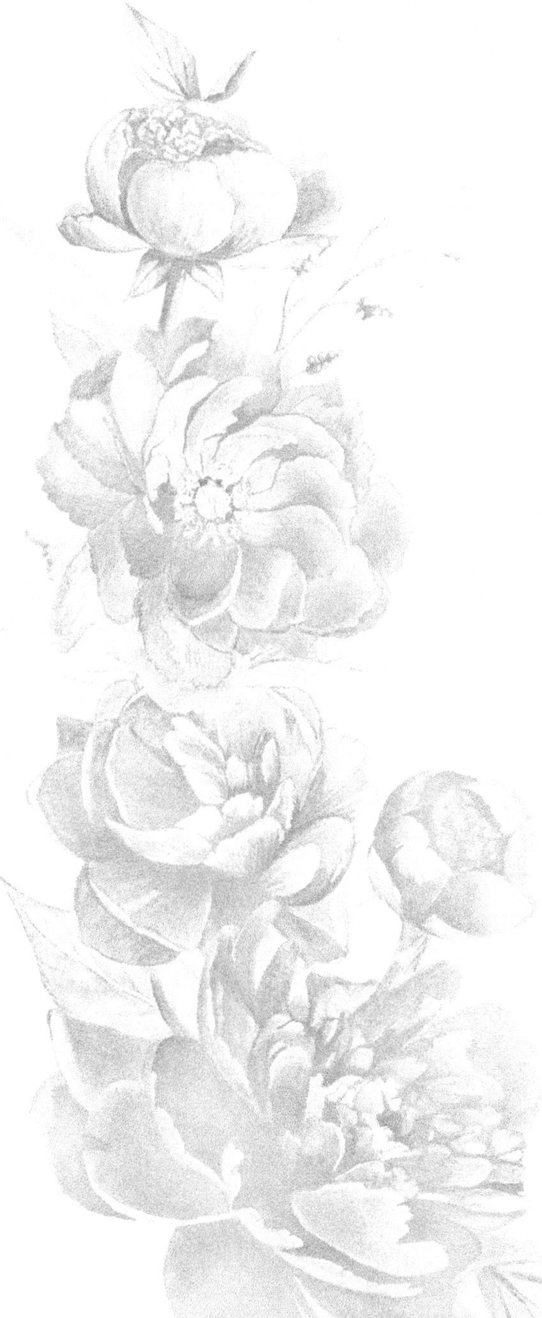

This book belongs to

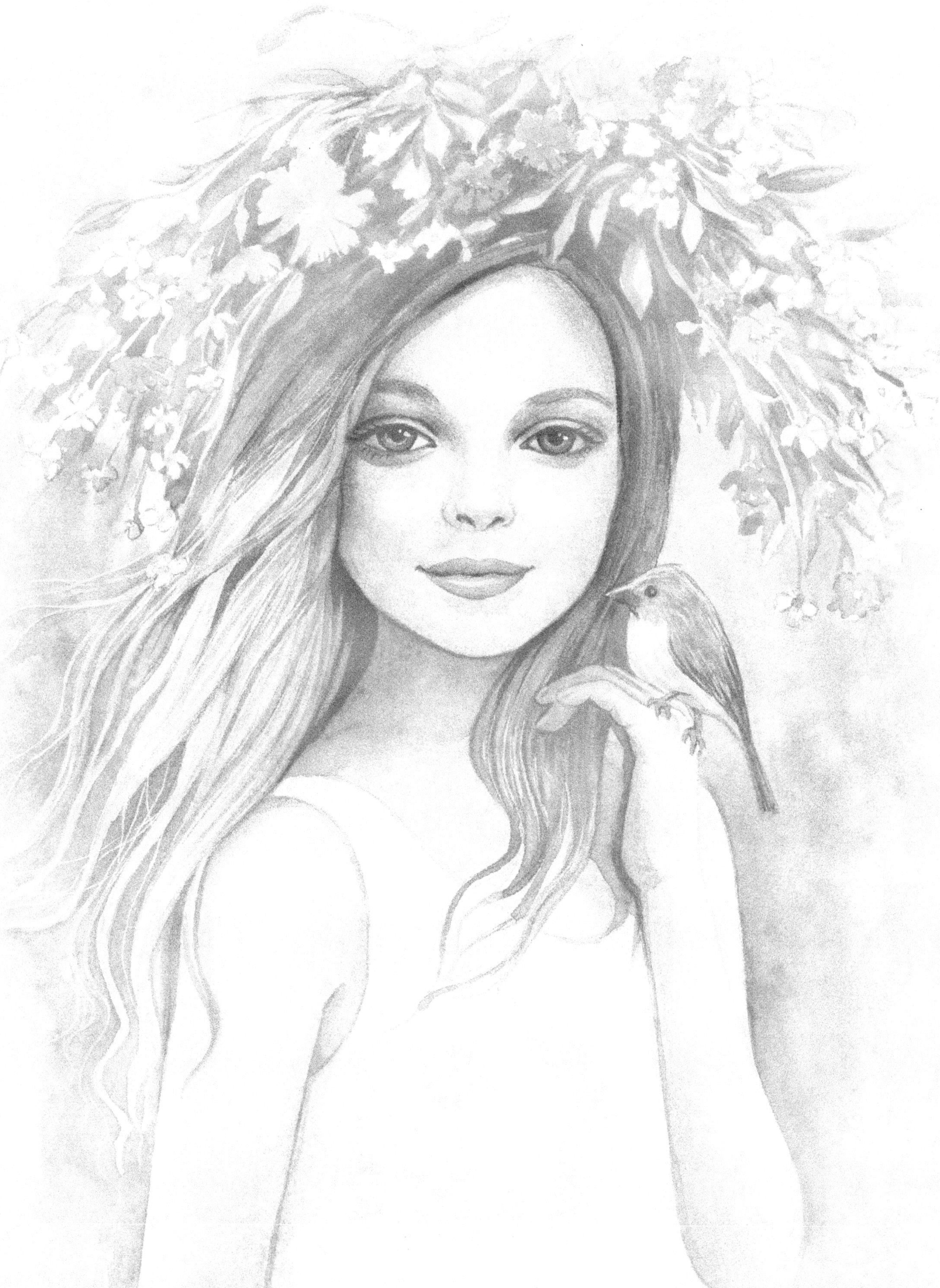

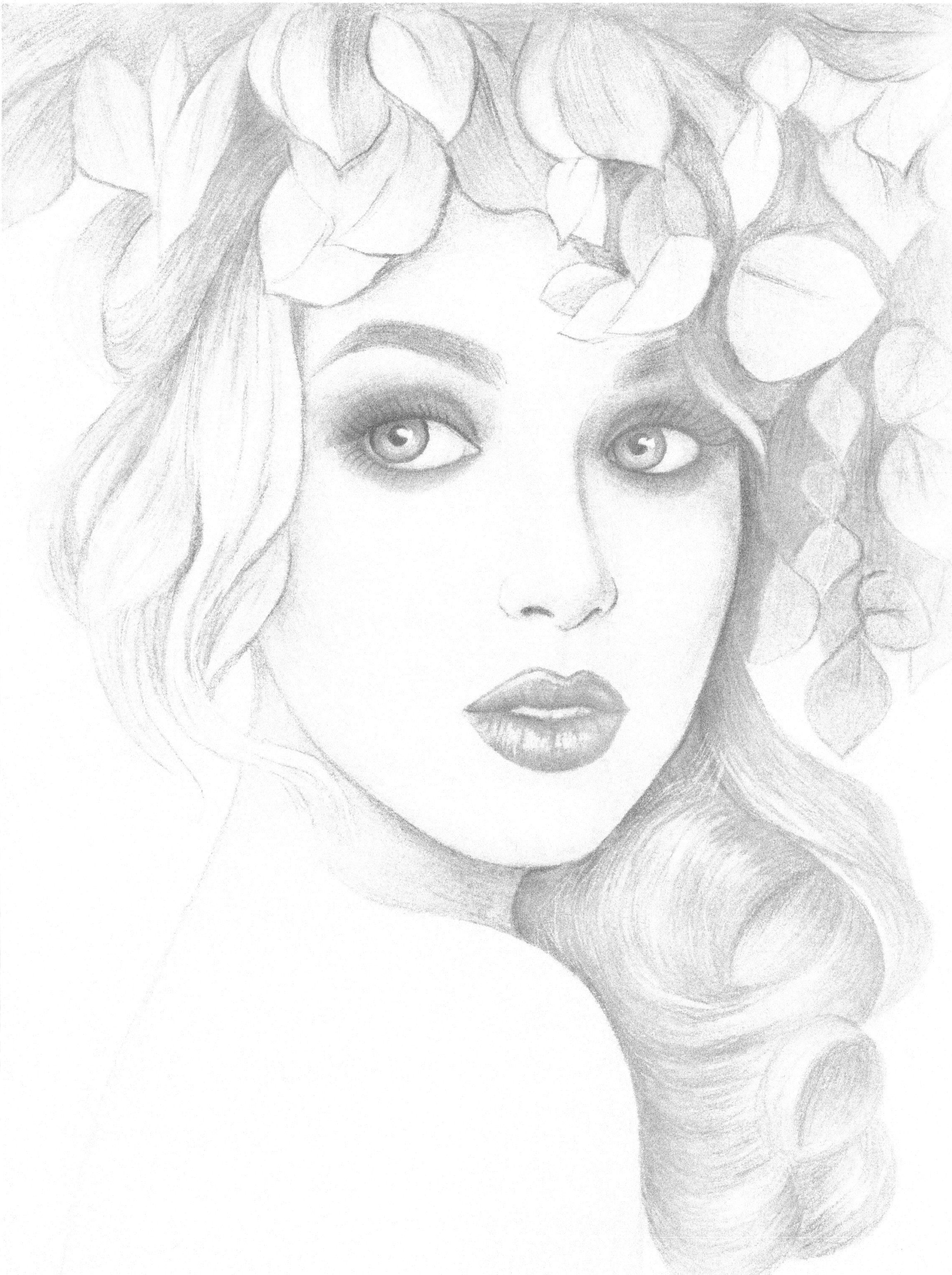

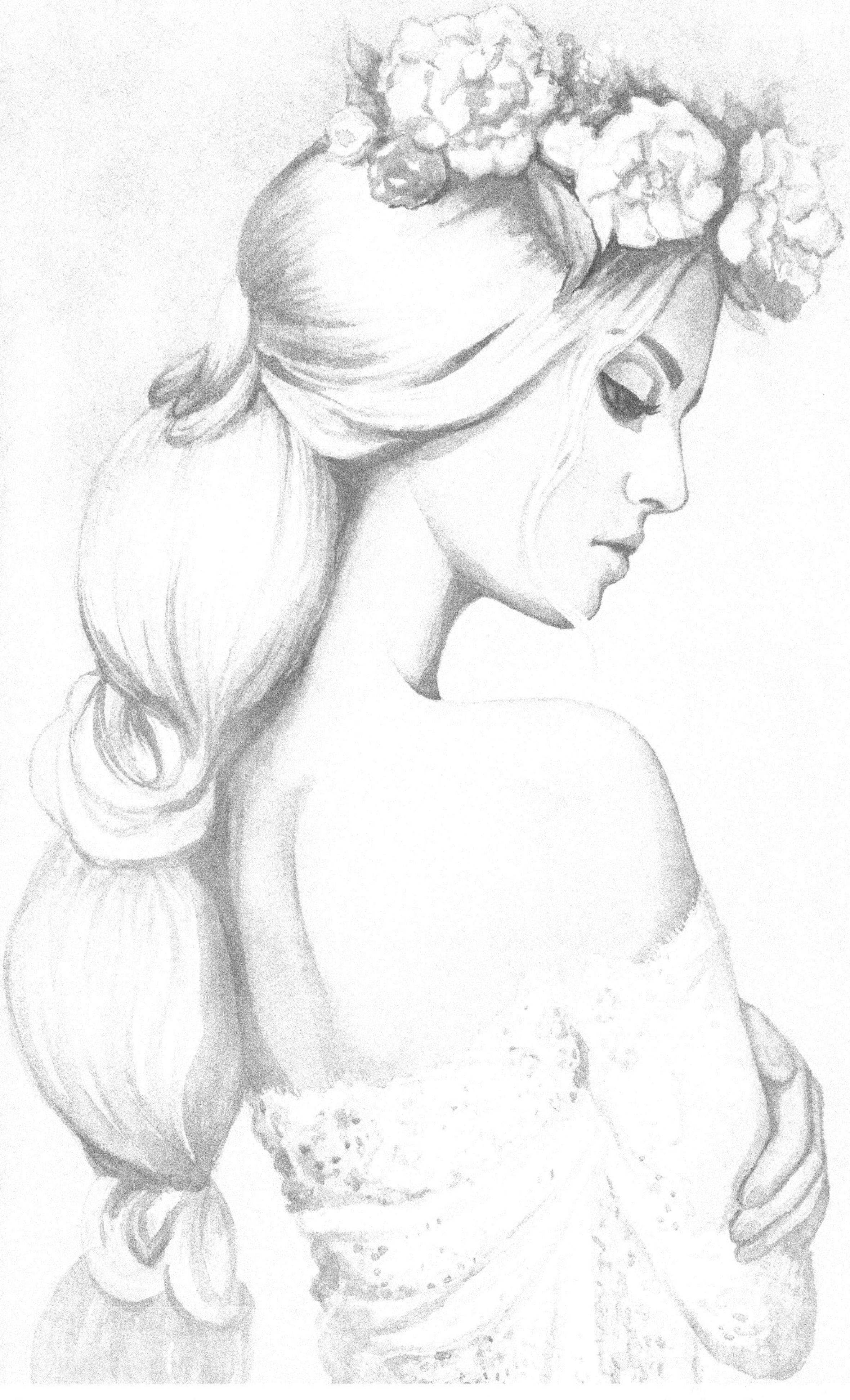

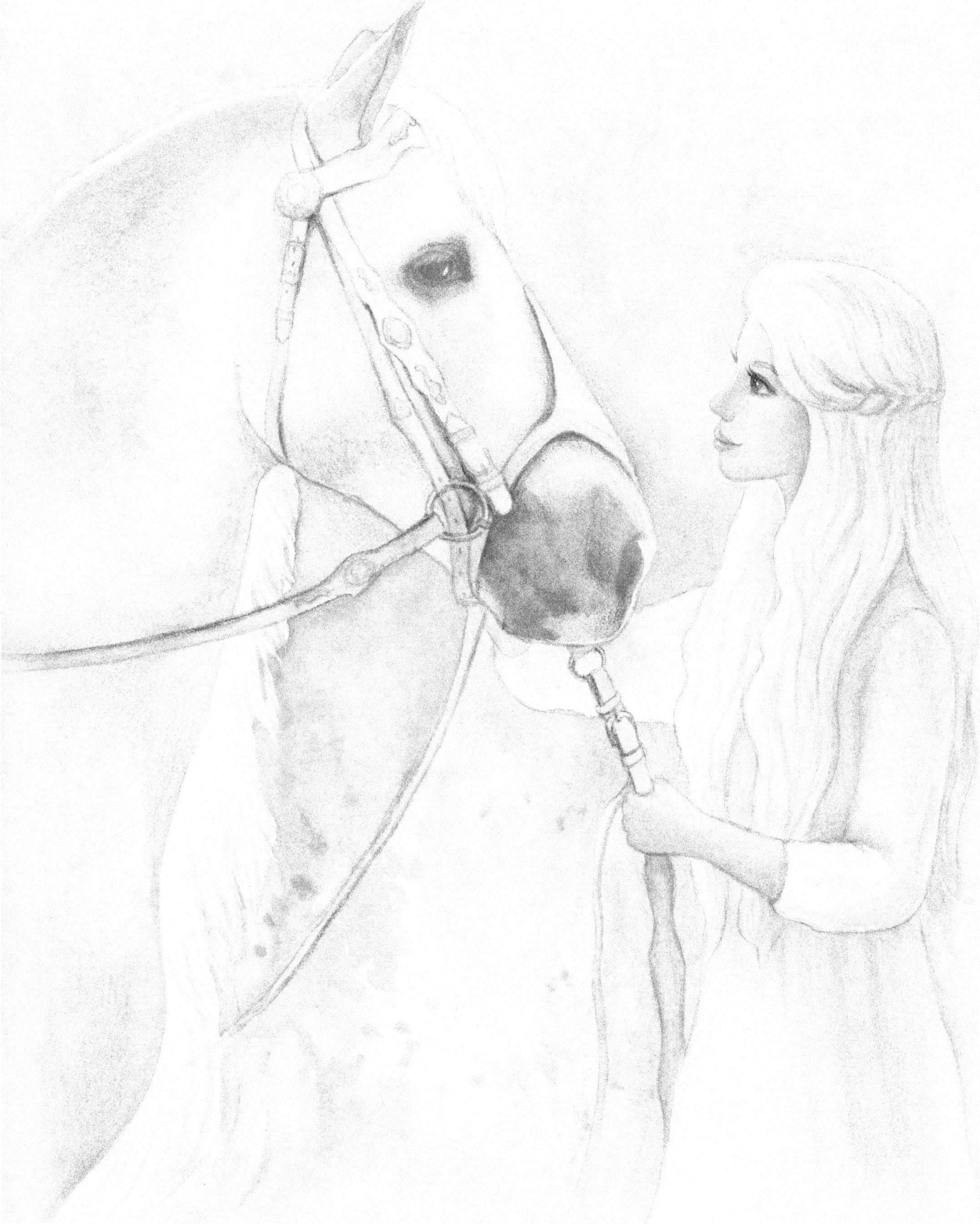

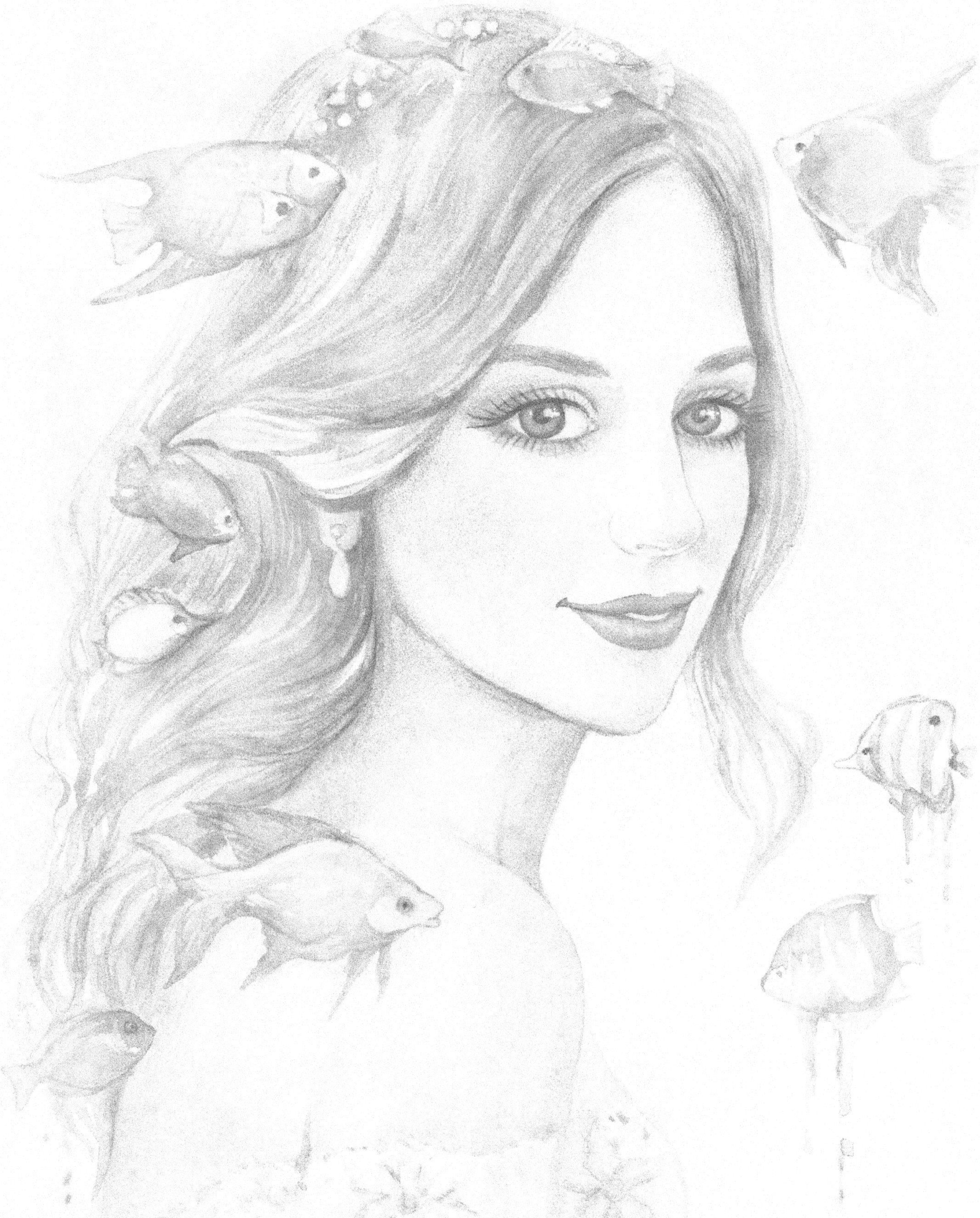

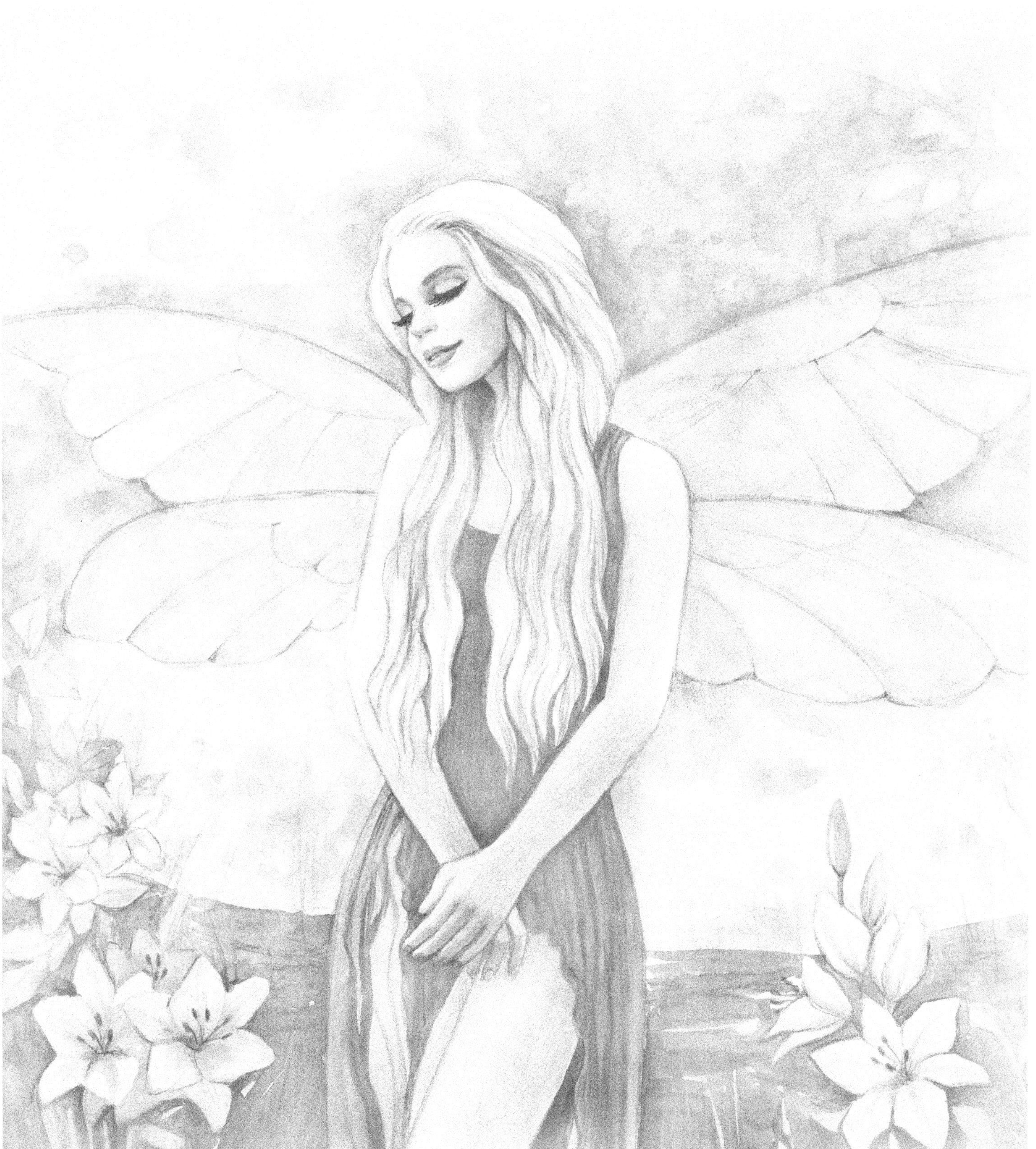

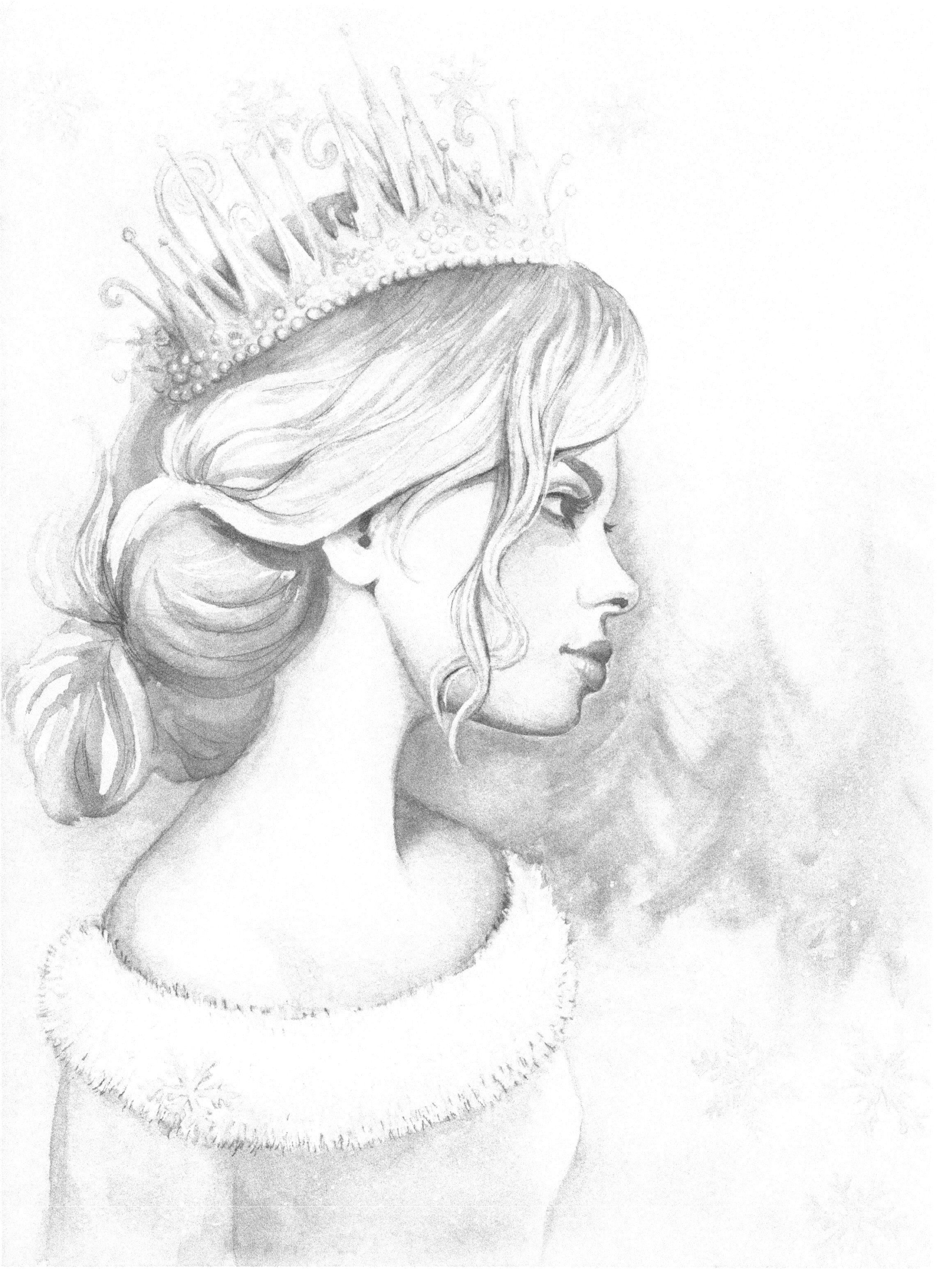

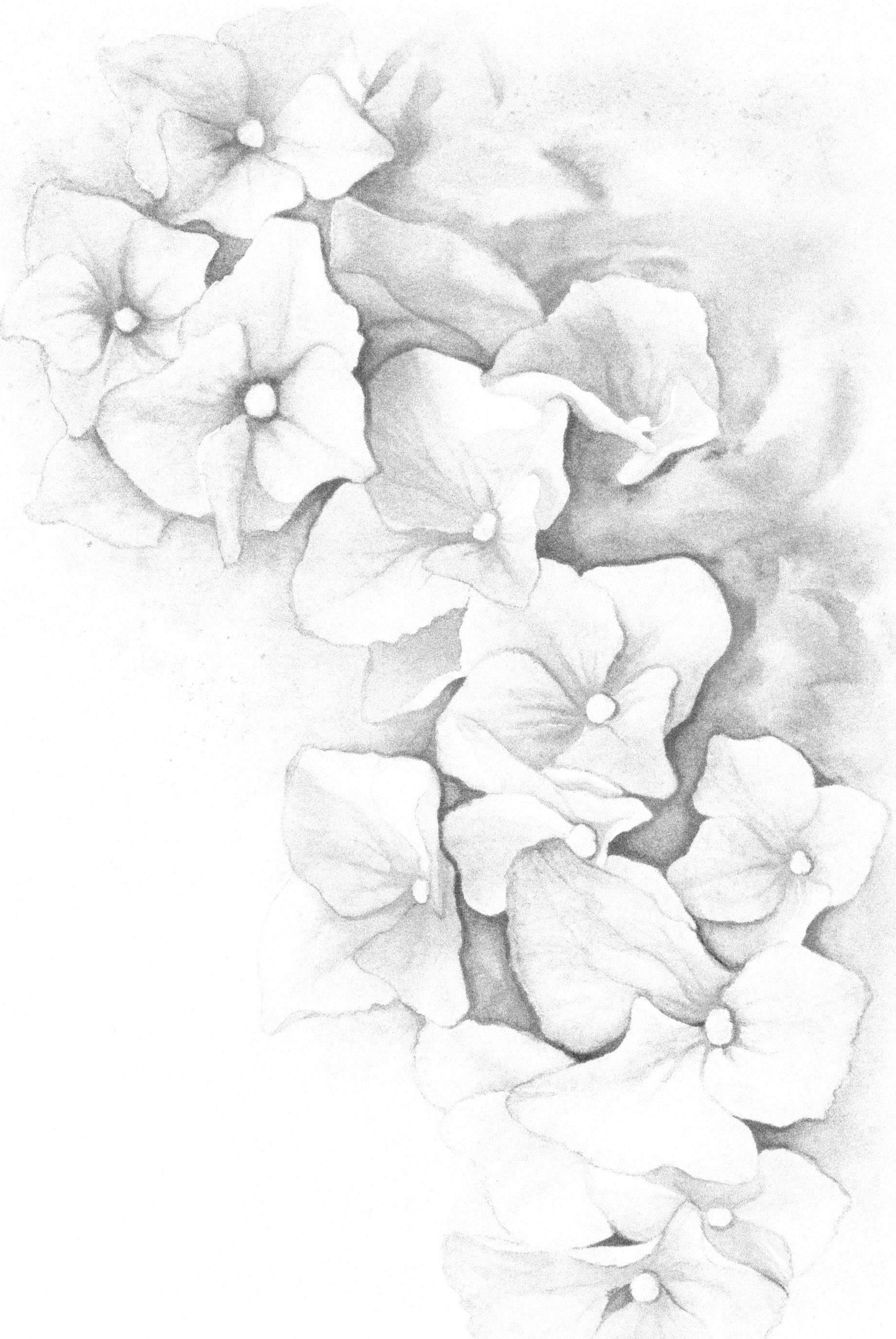

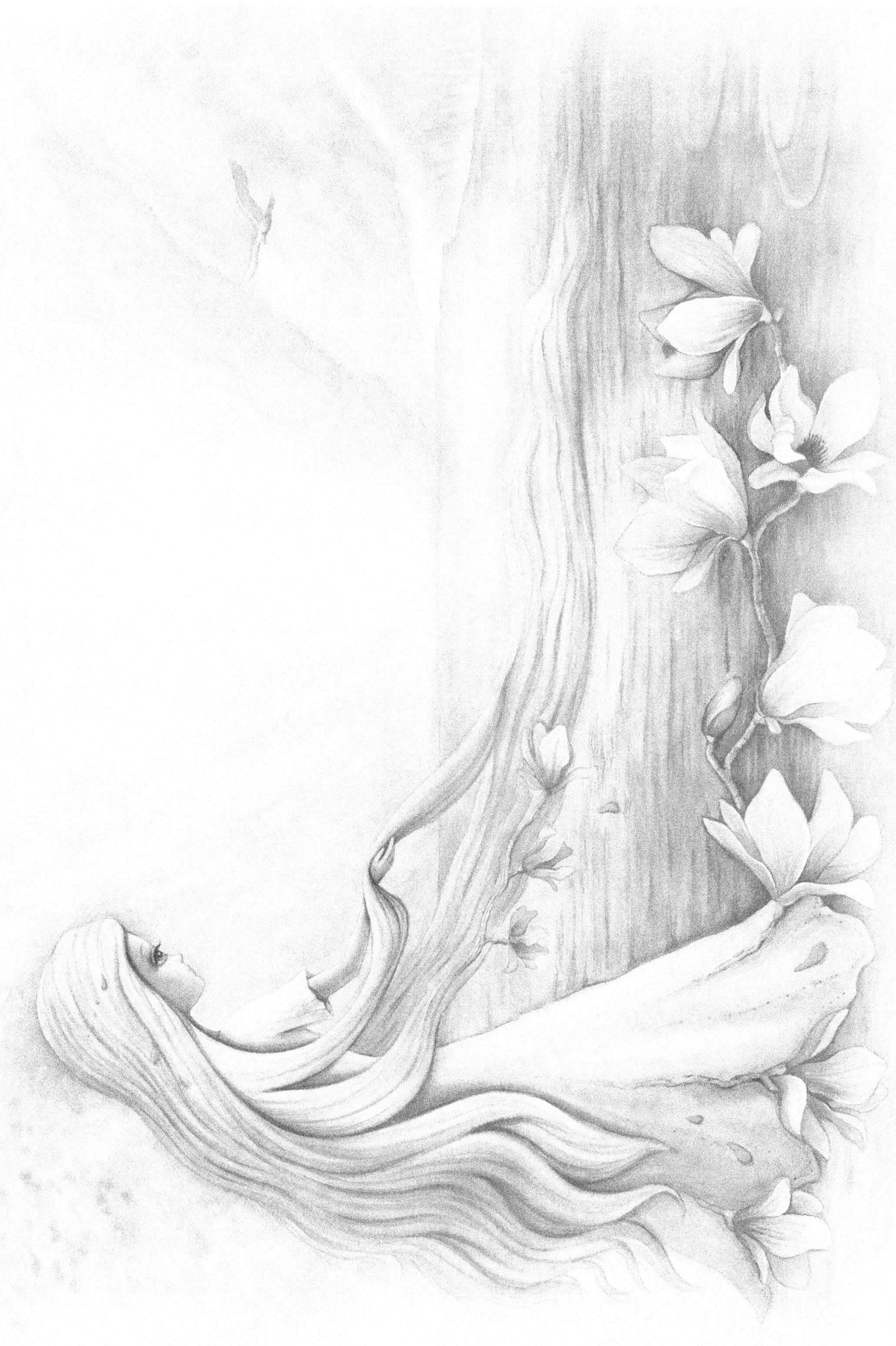

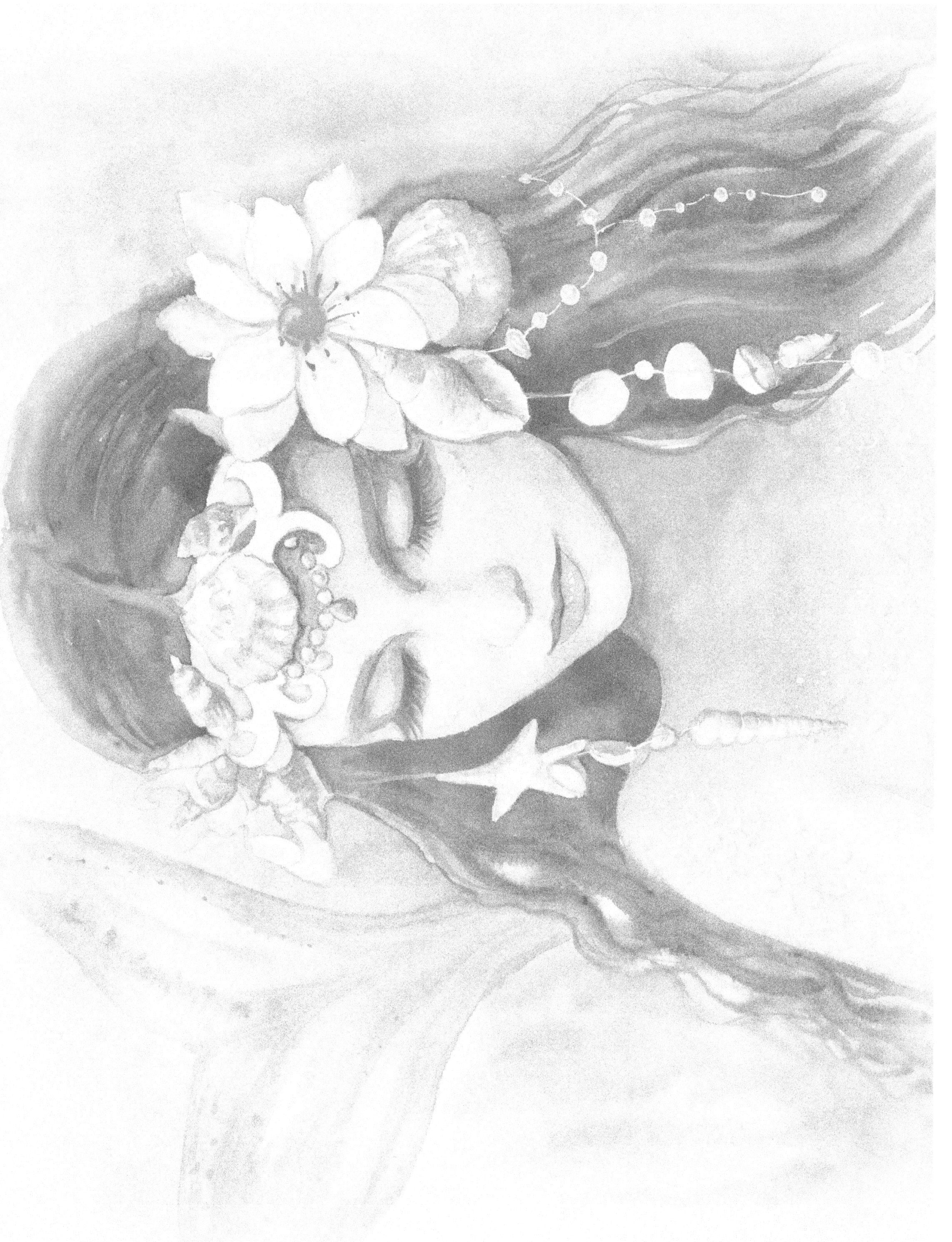

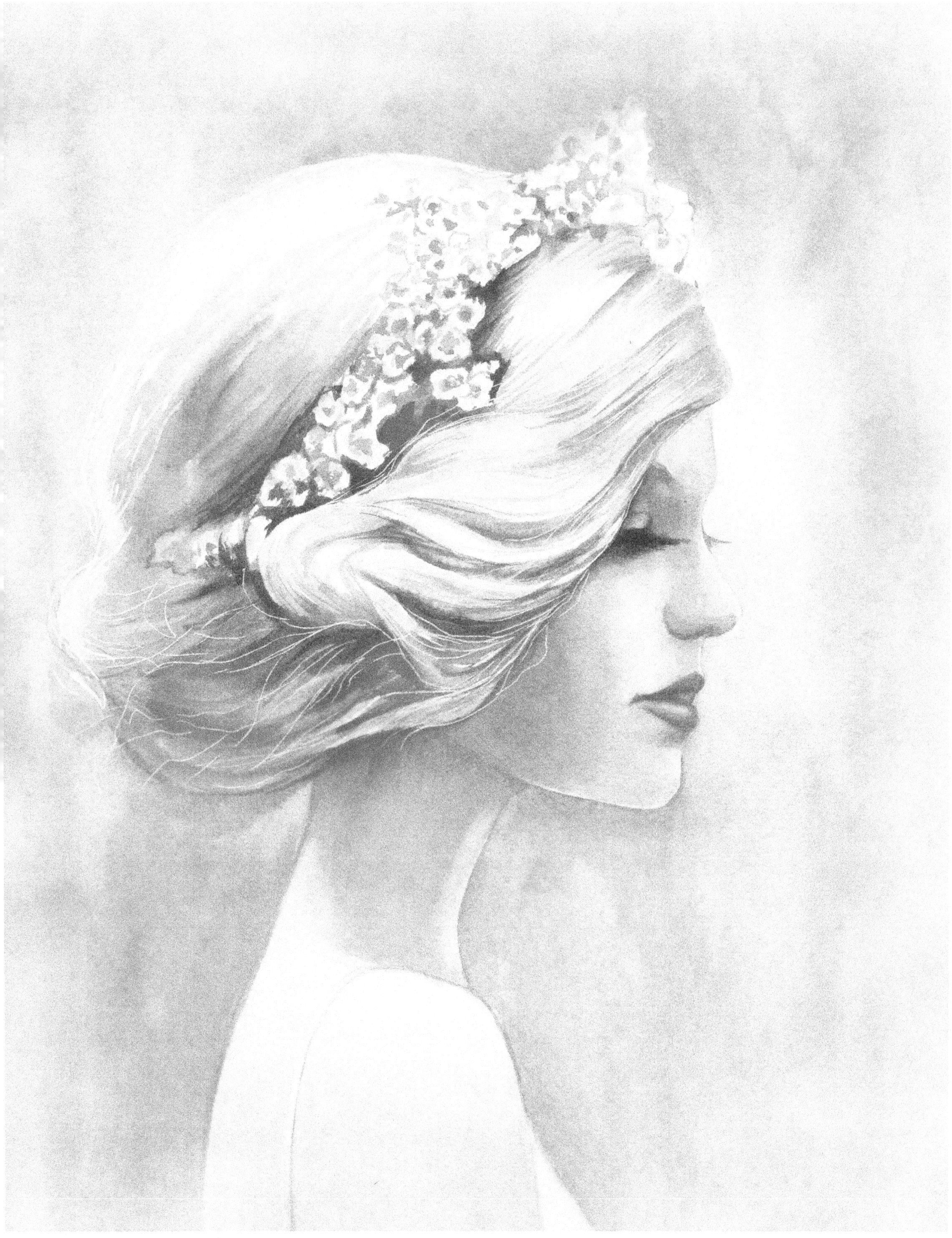

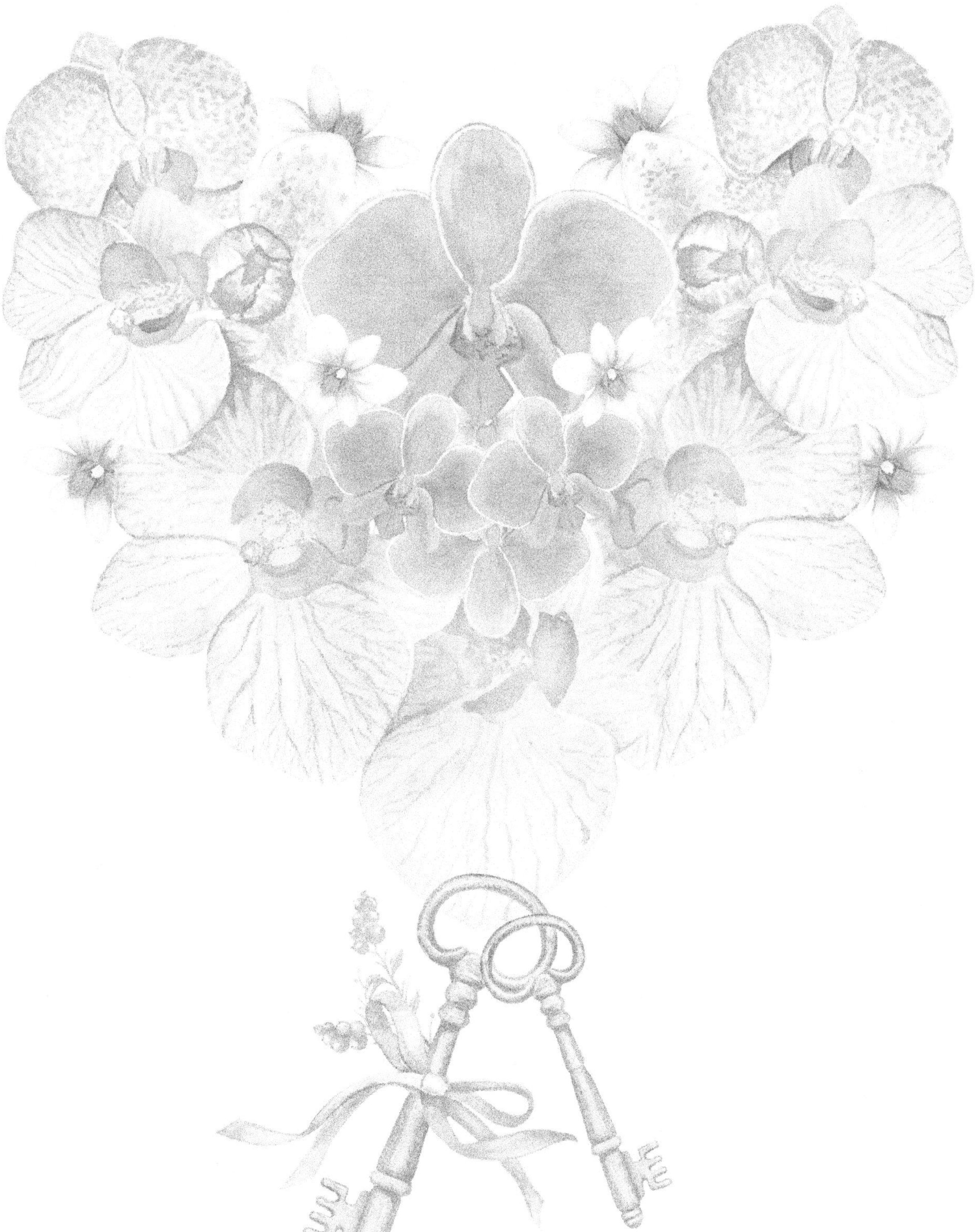

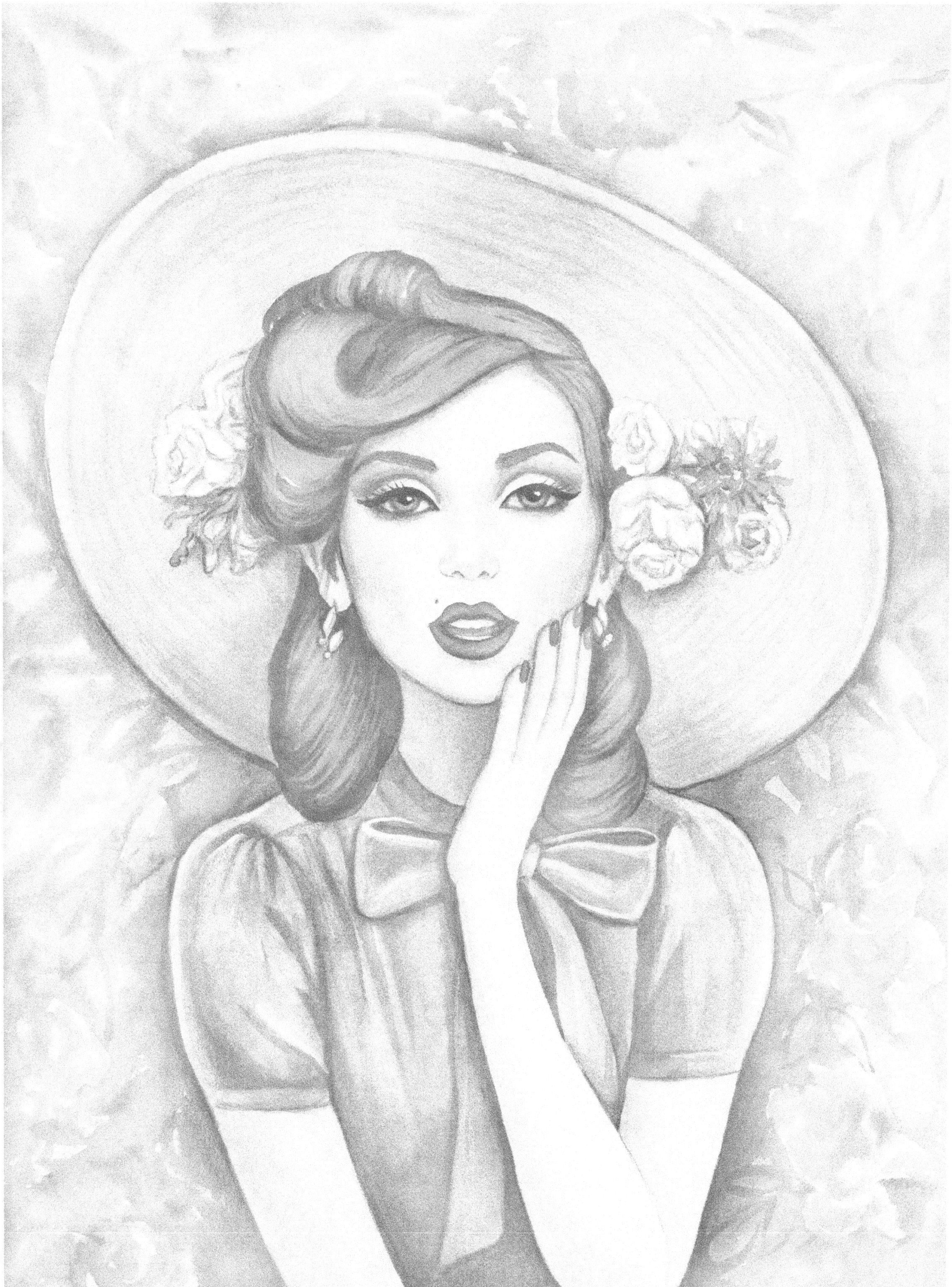

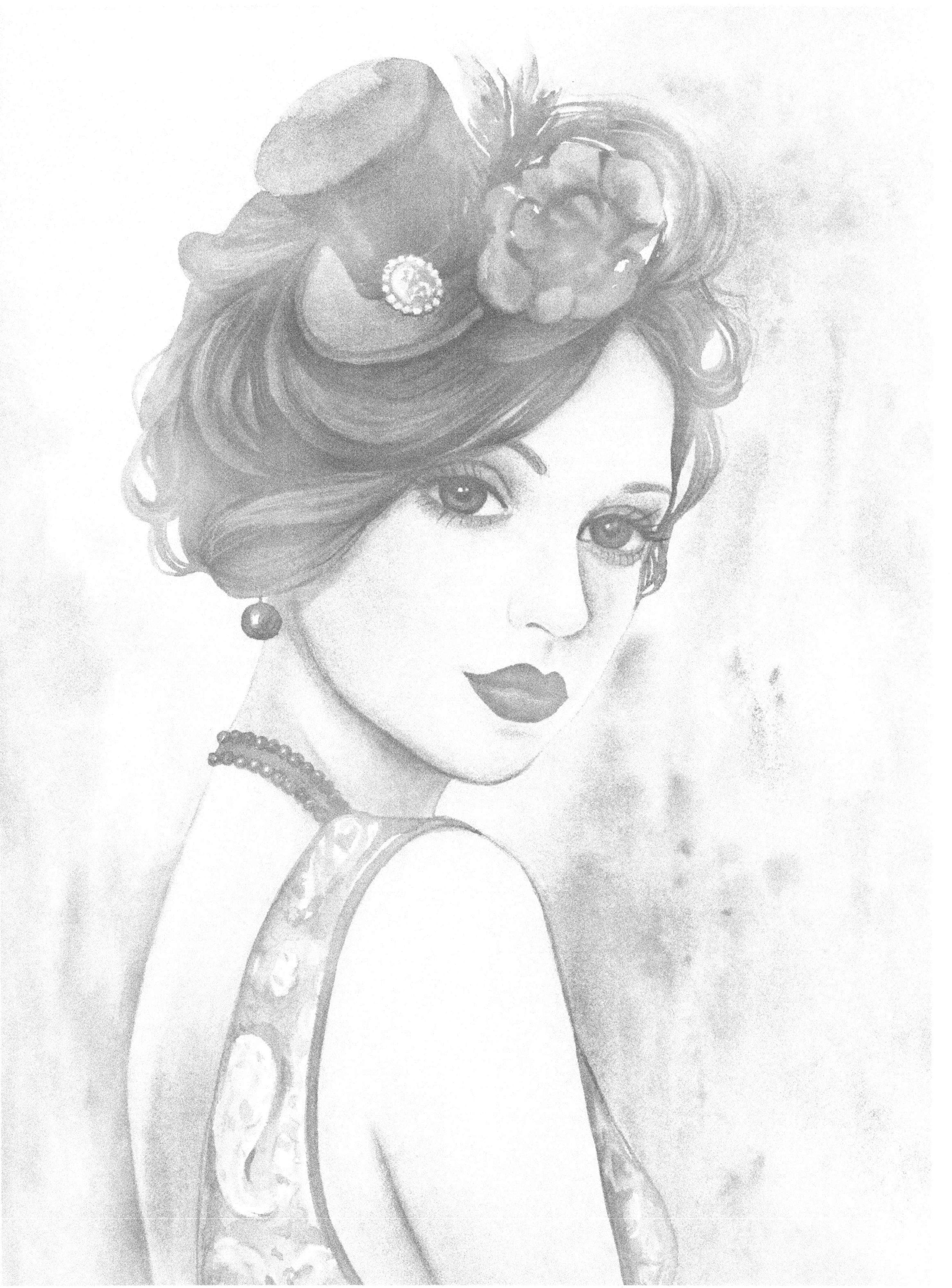

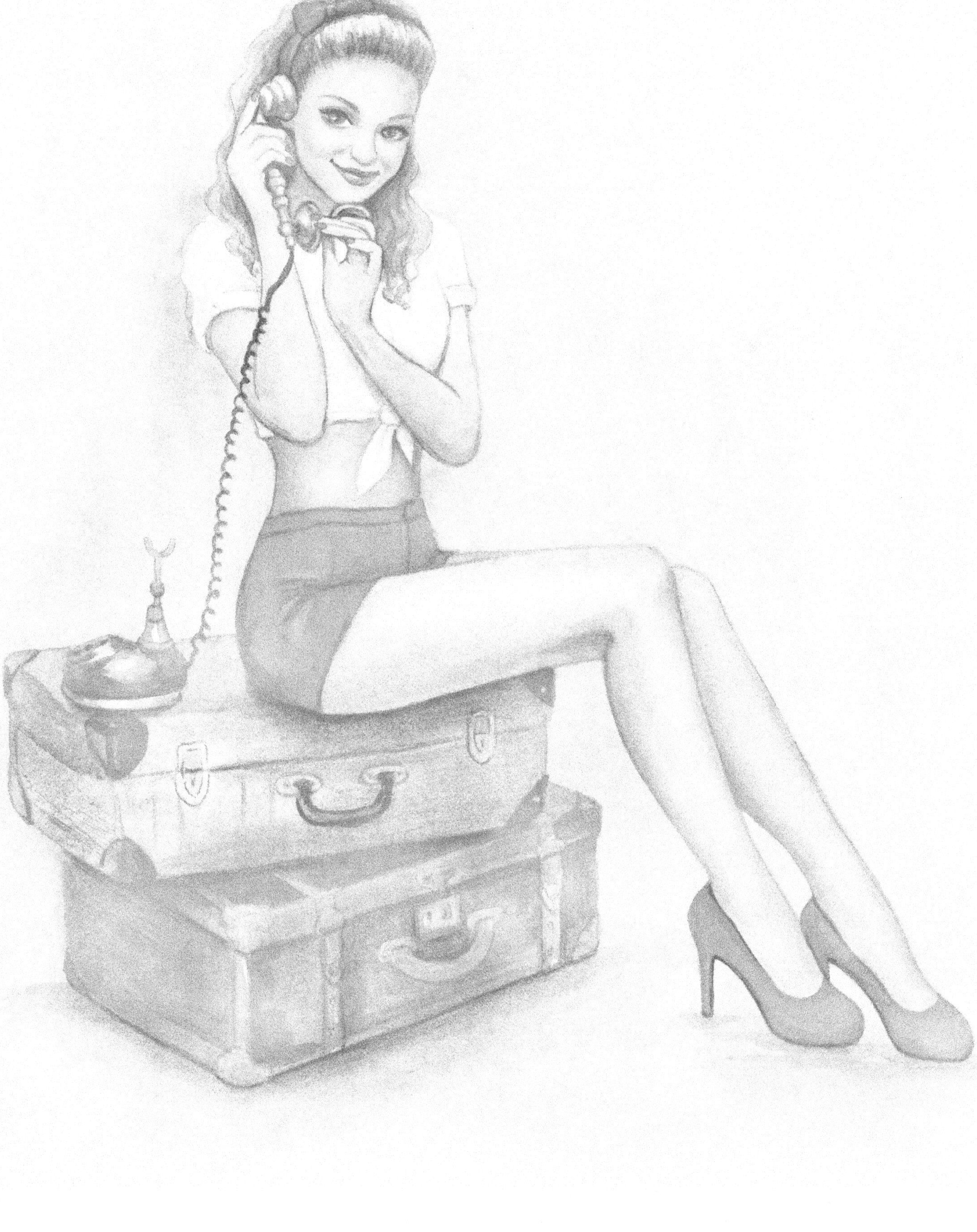

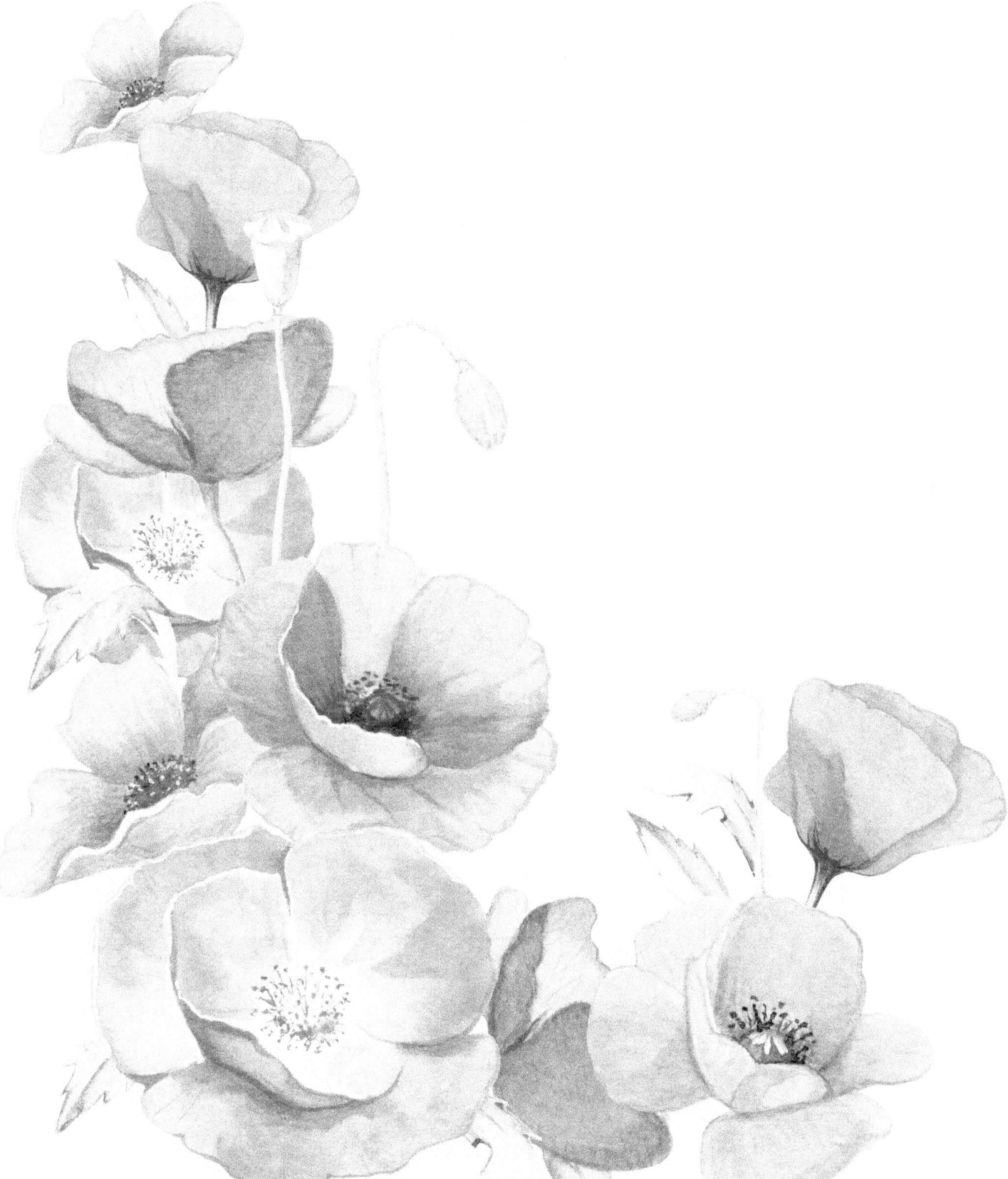

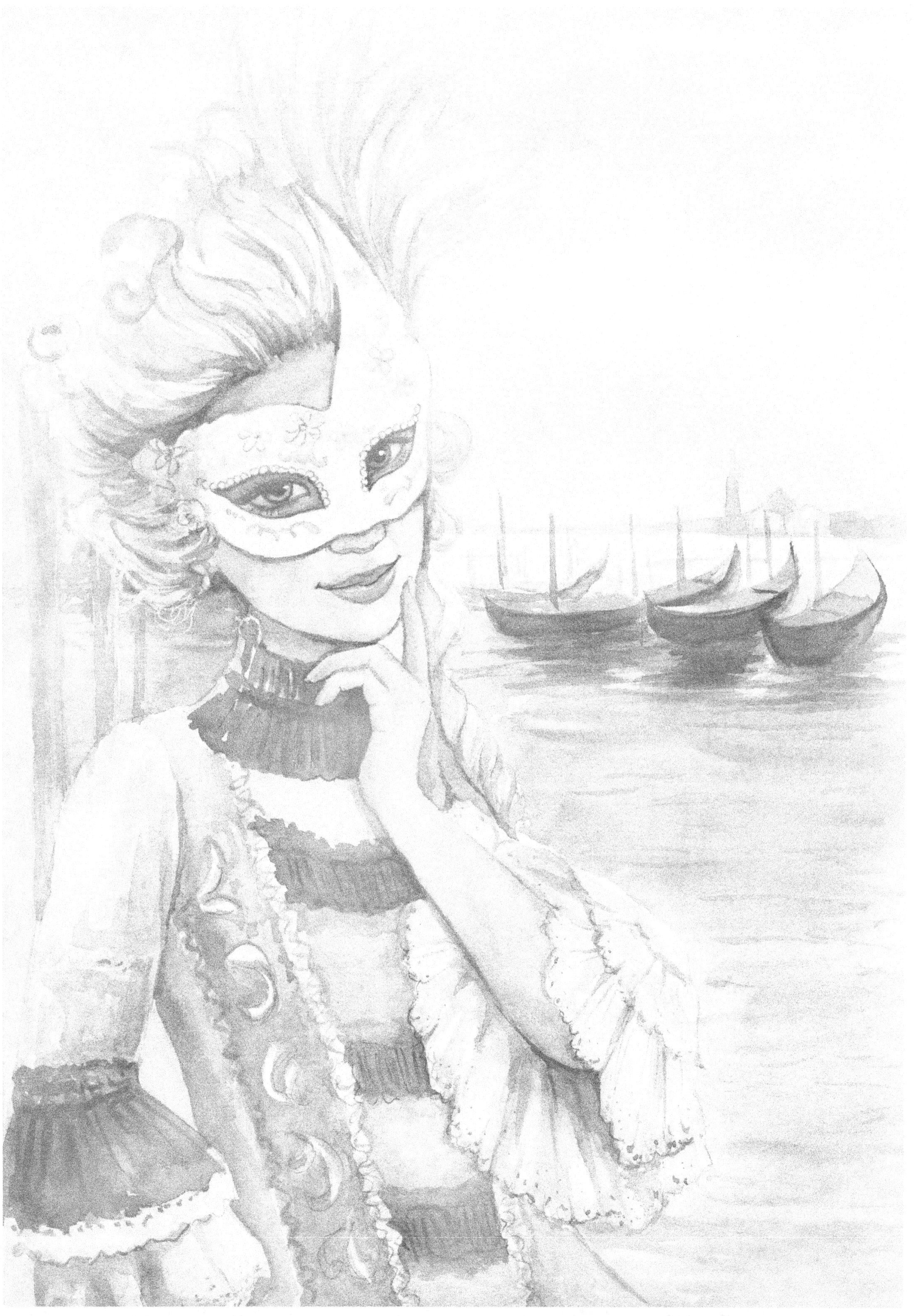

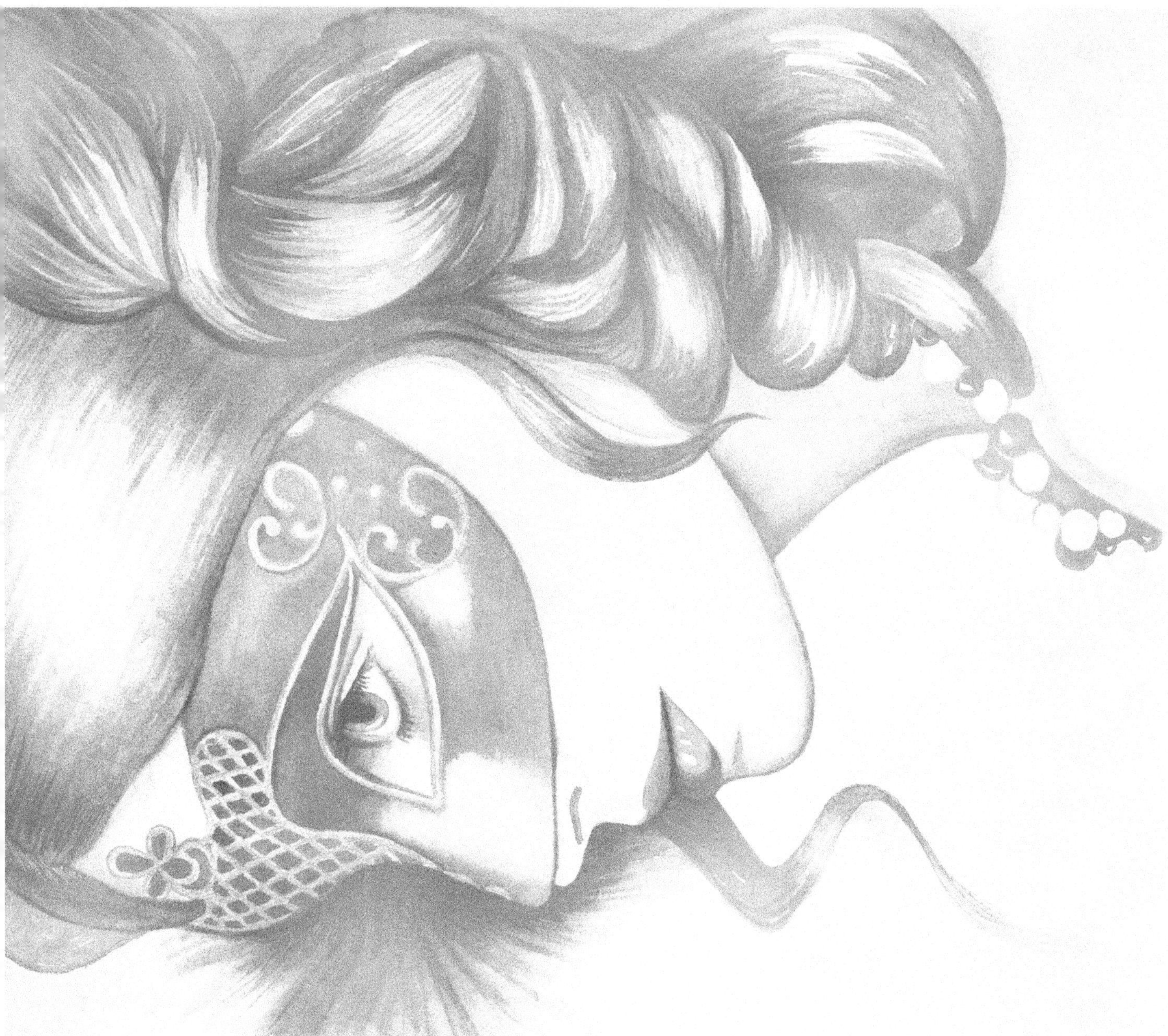

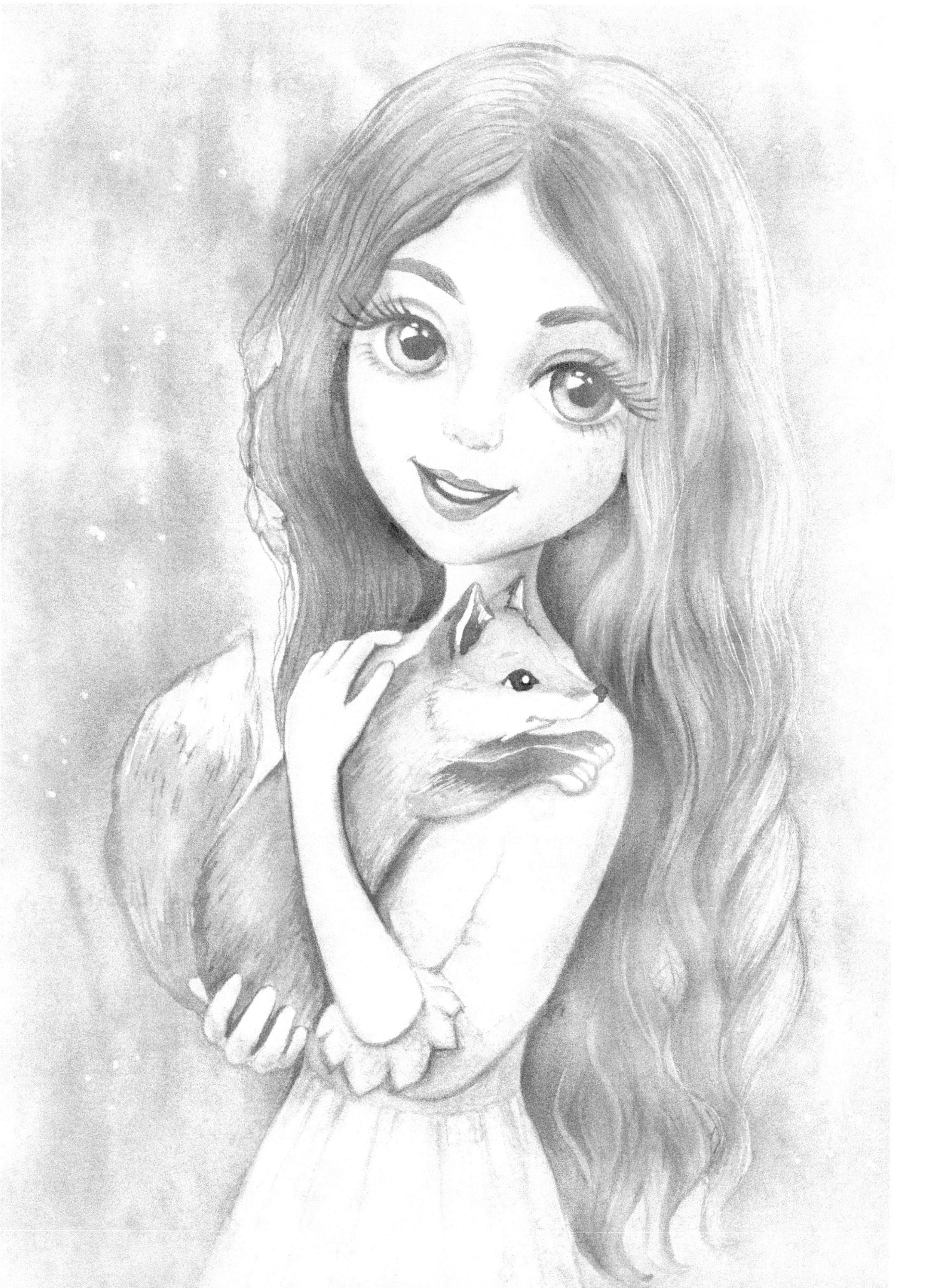

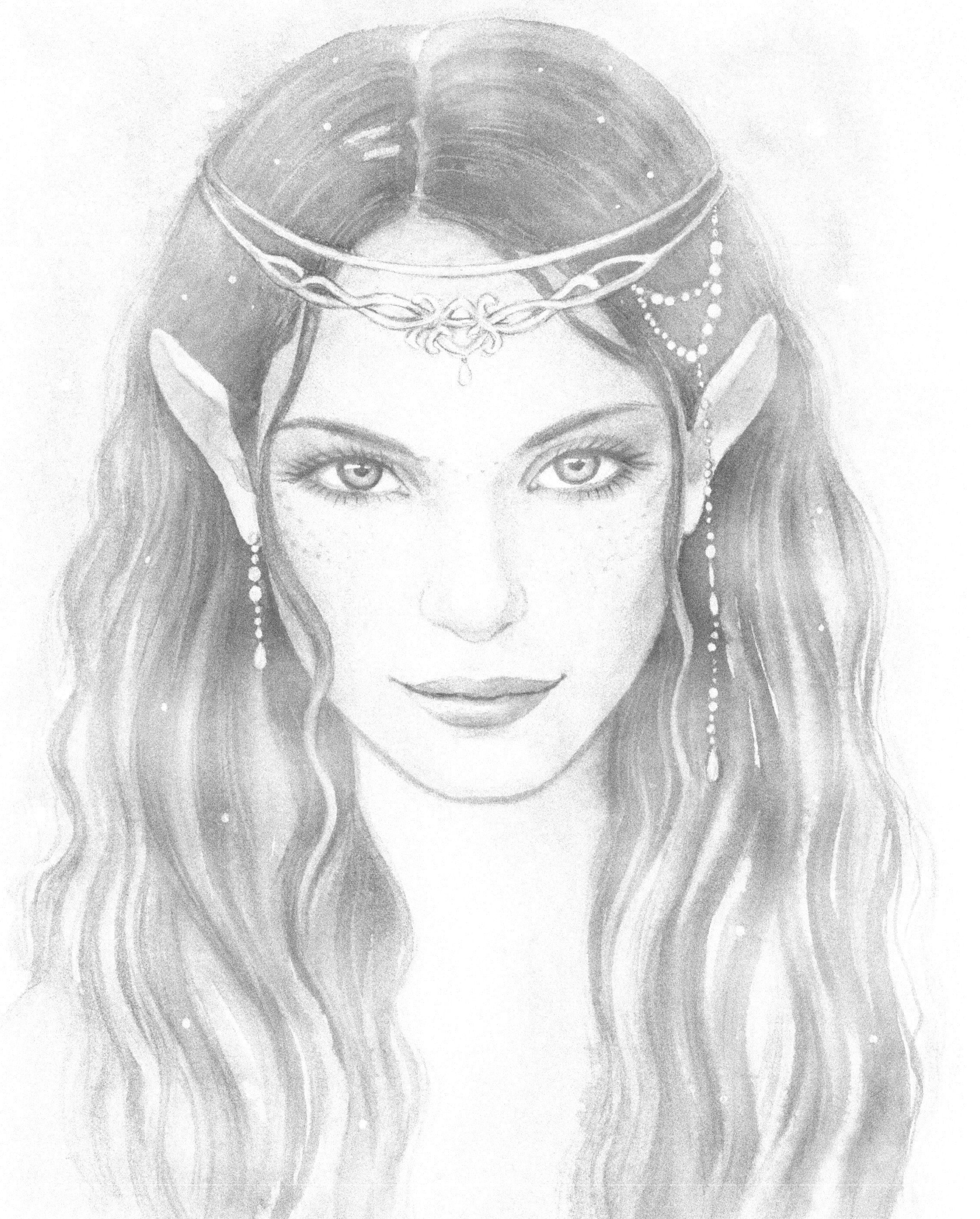

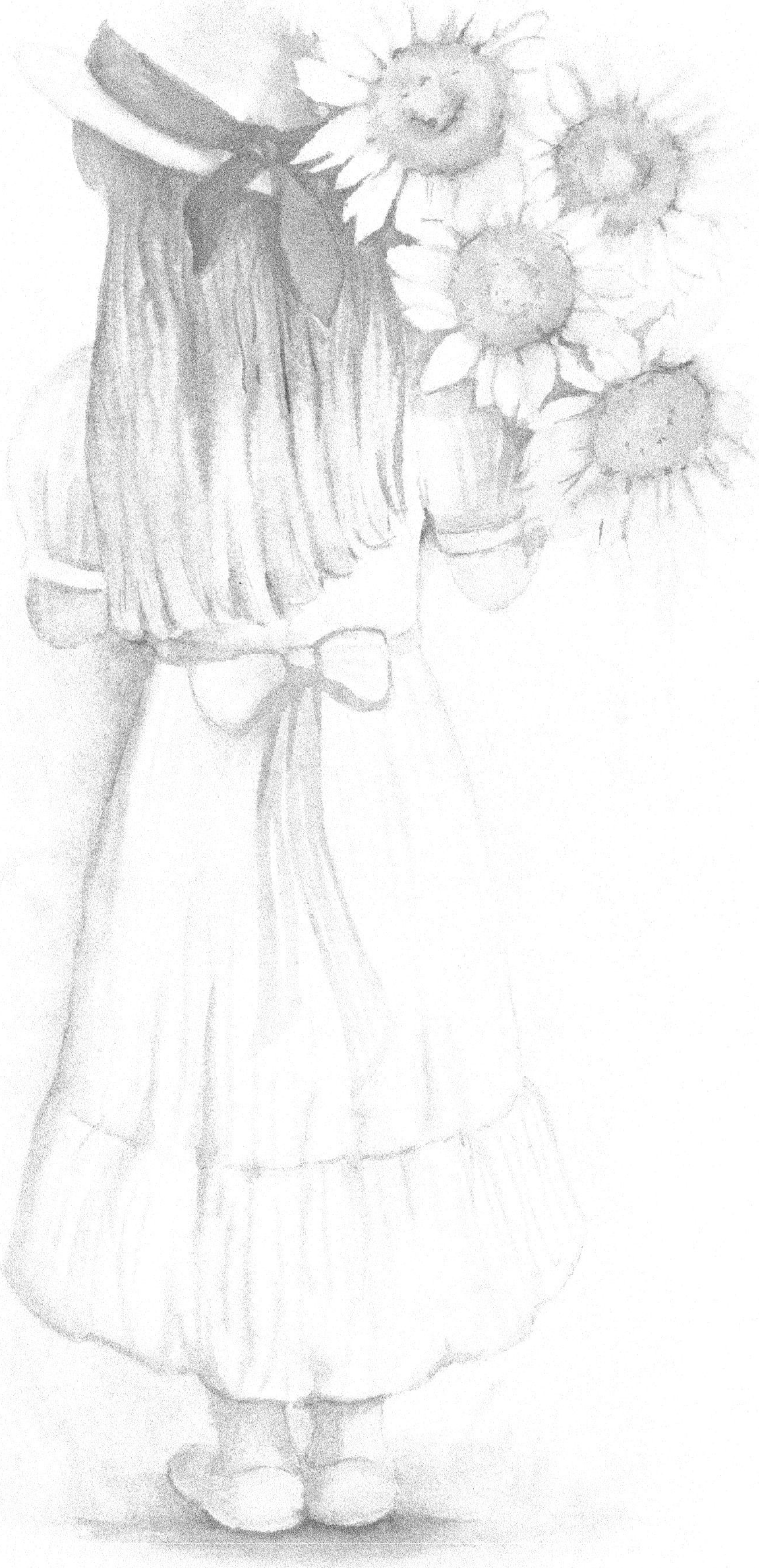

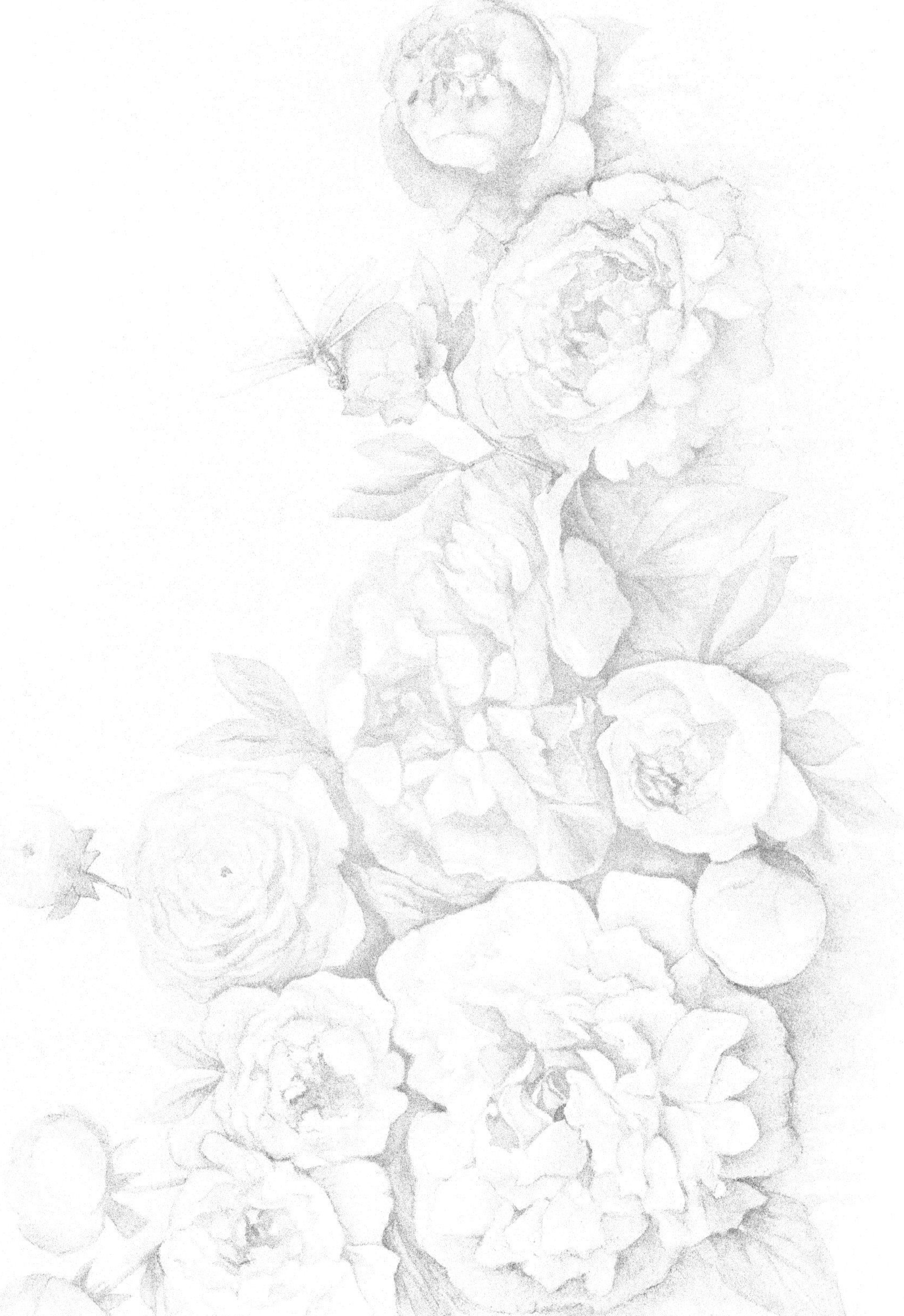

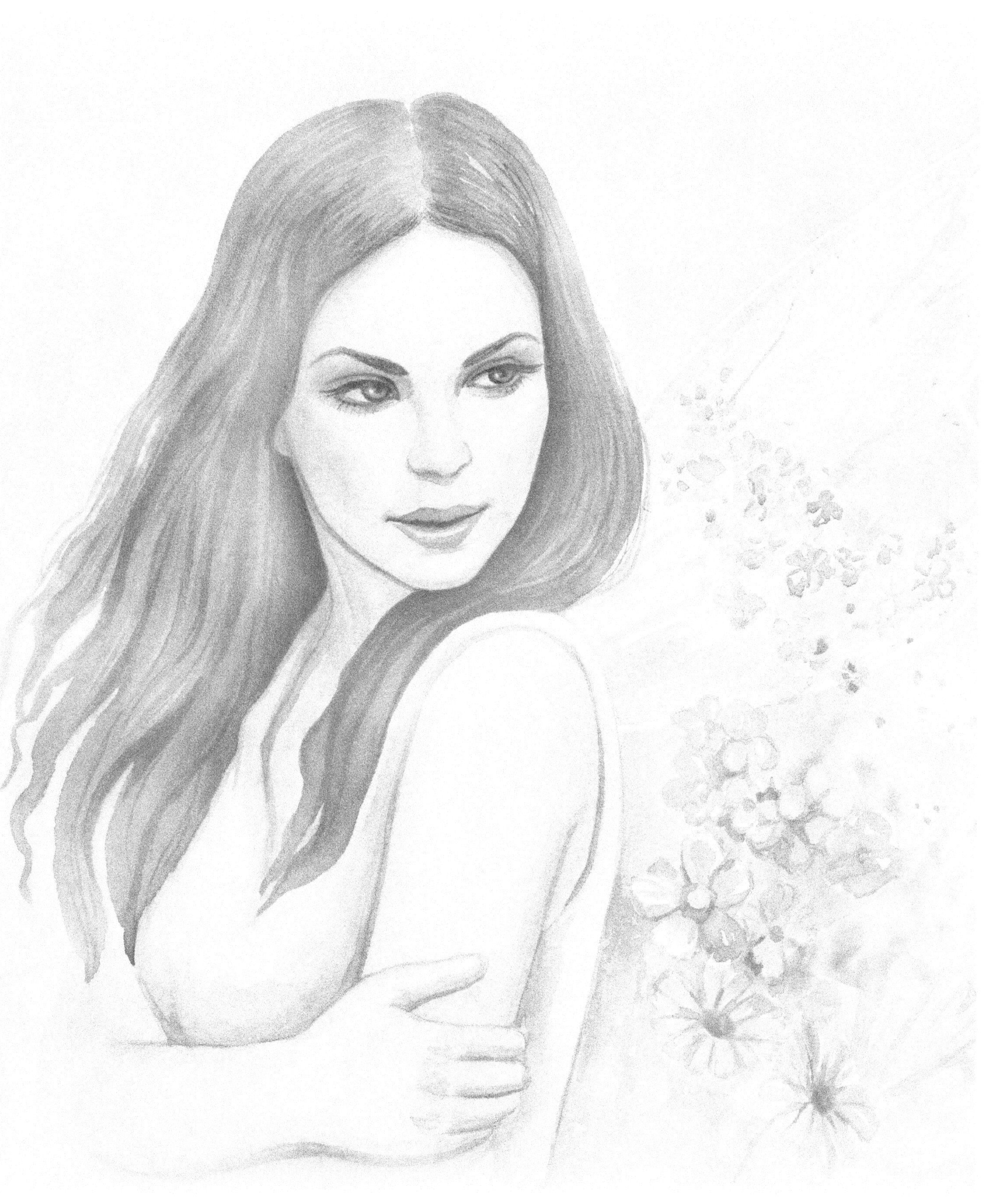

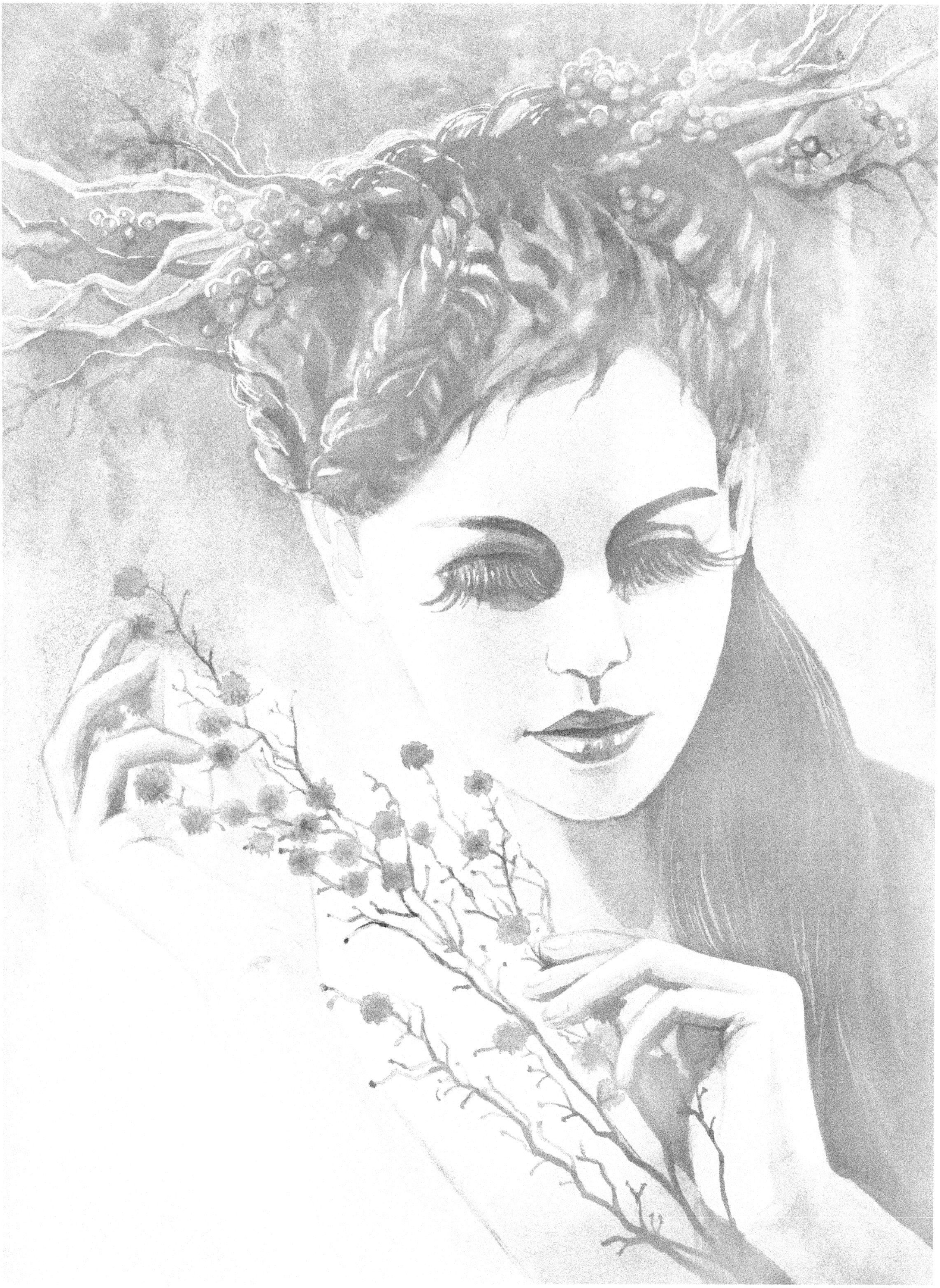

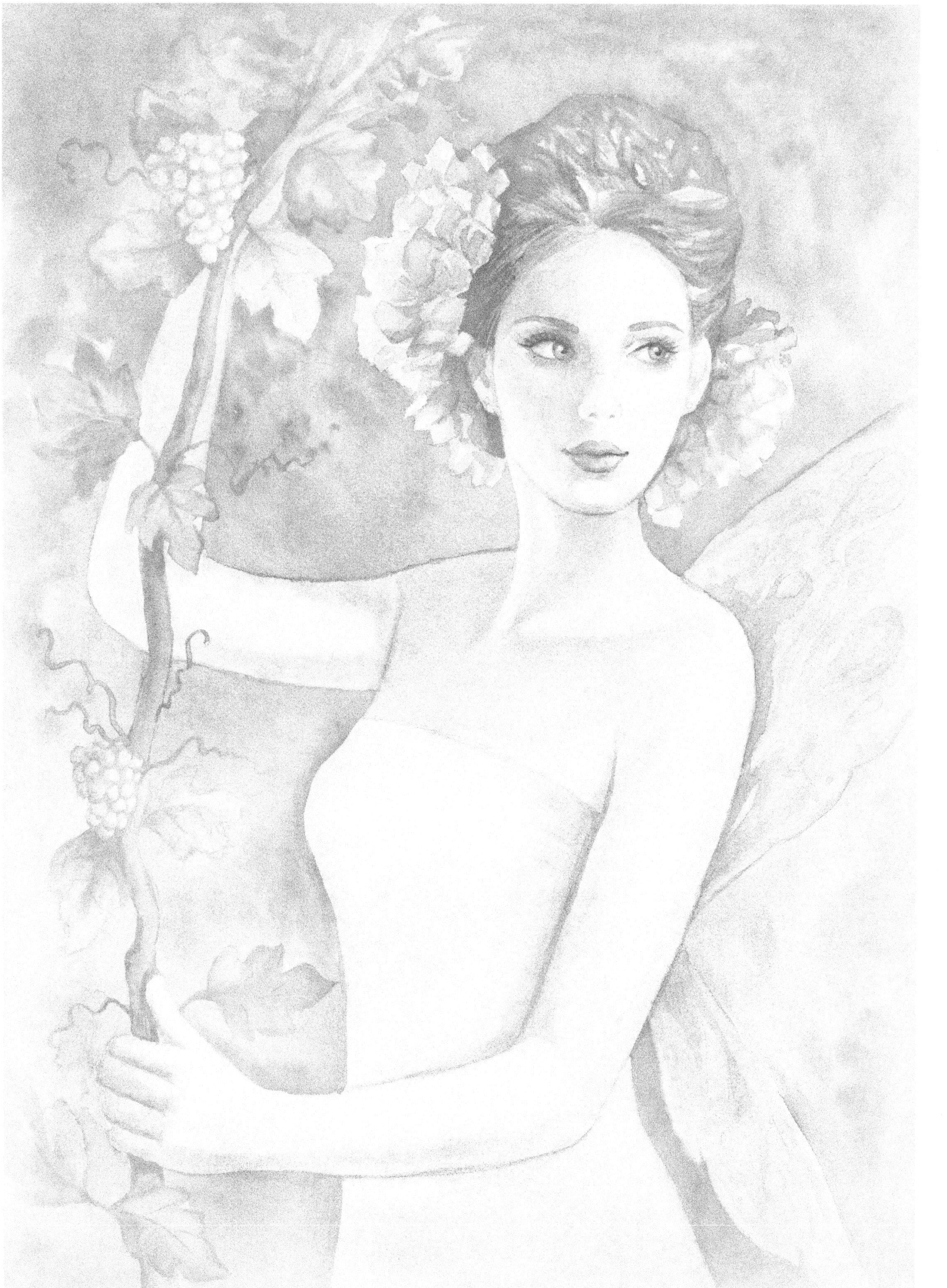

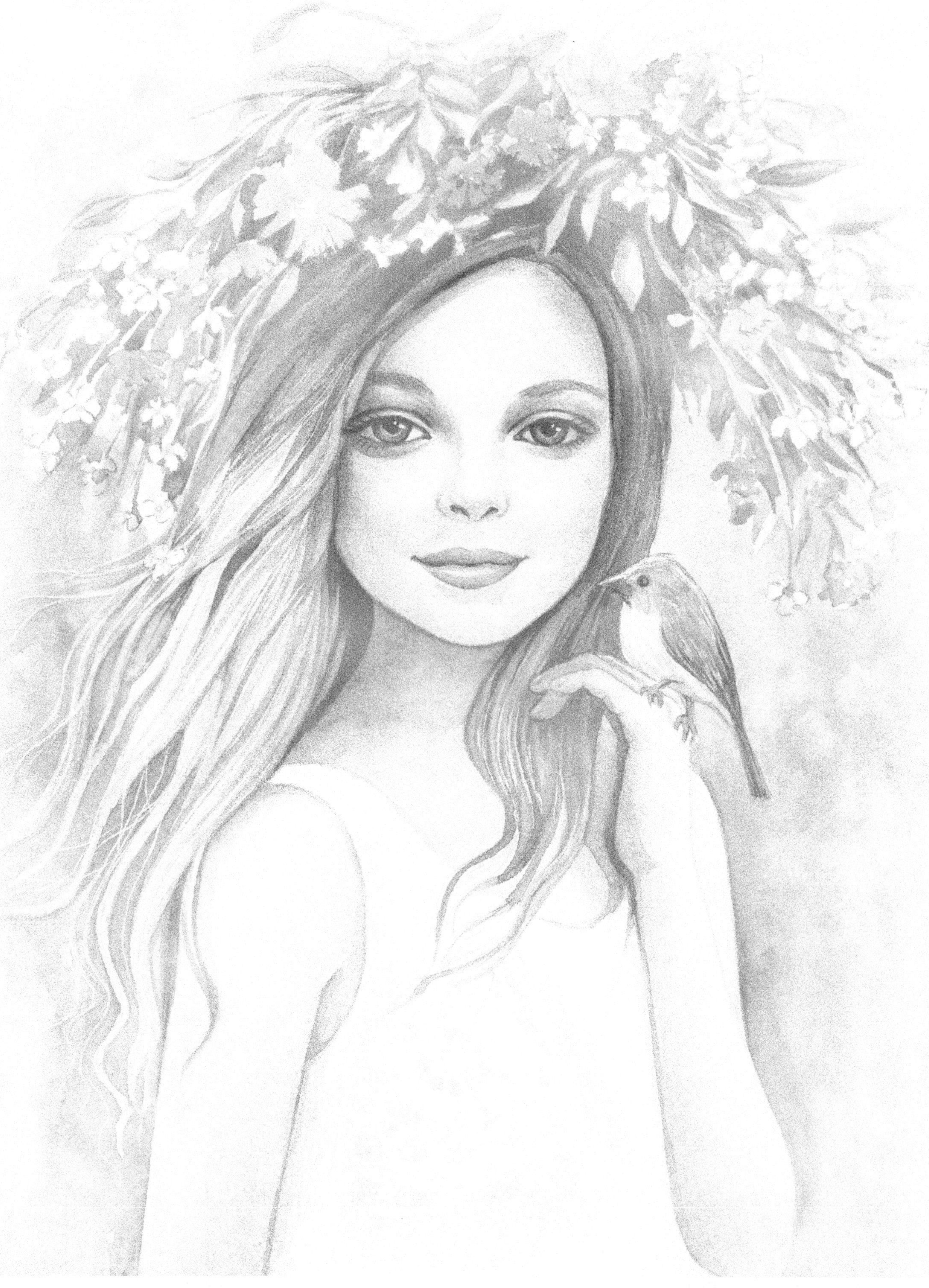

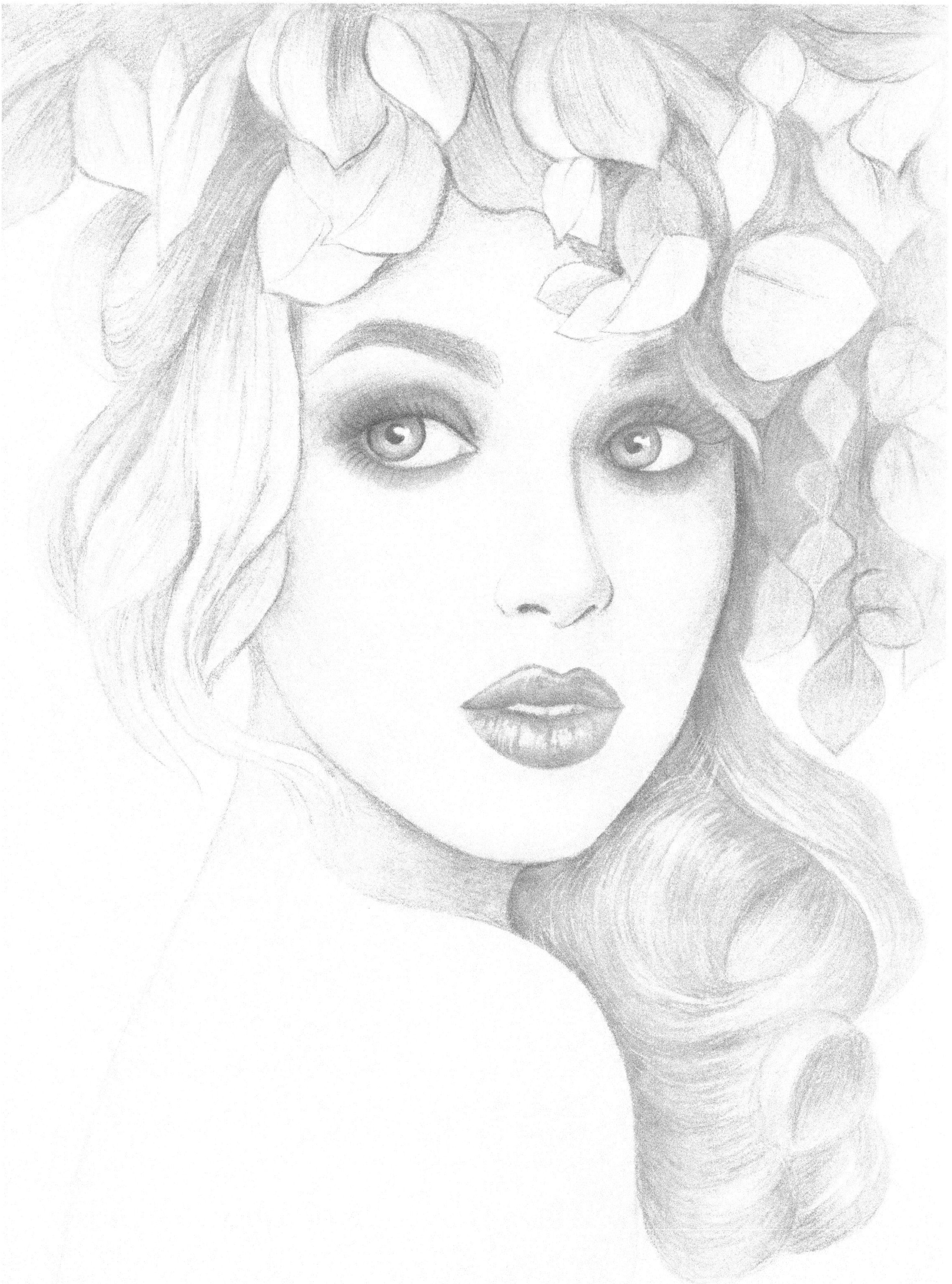

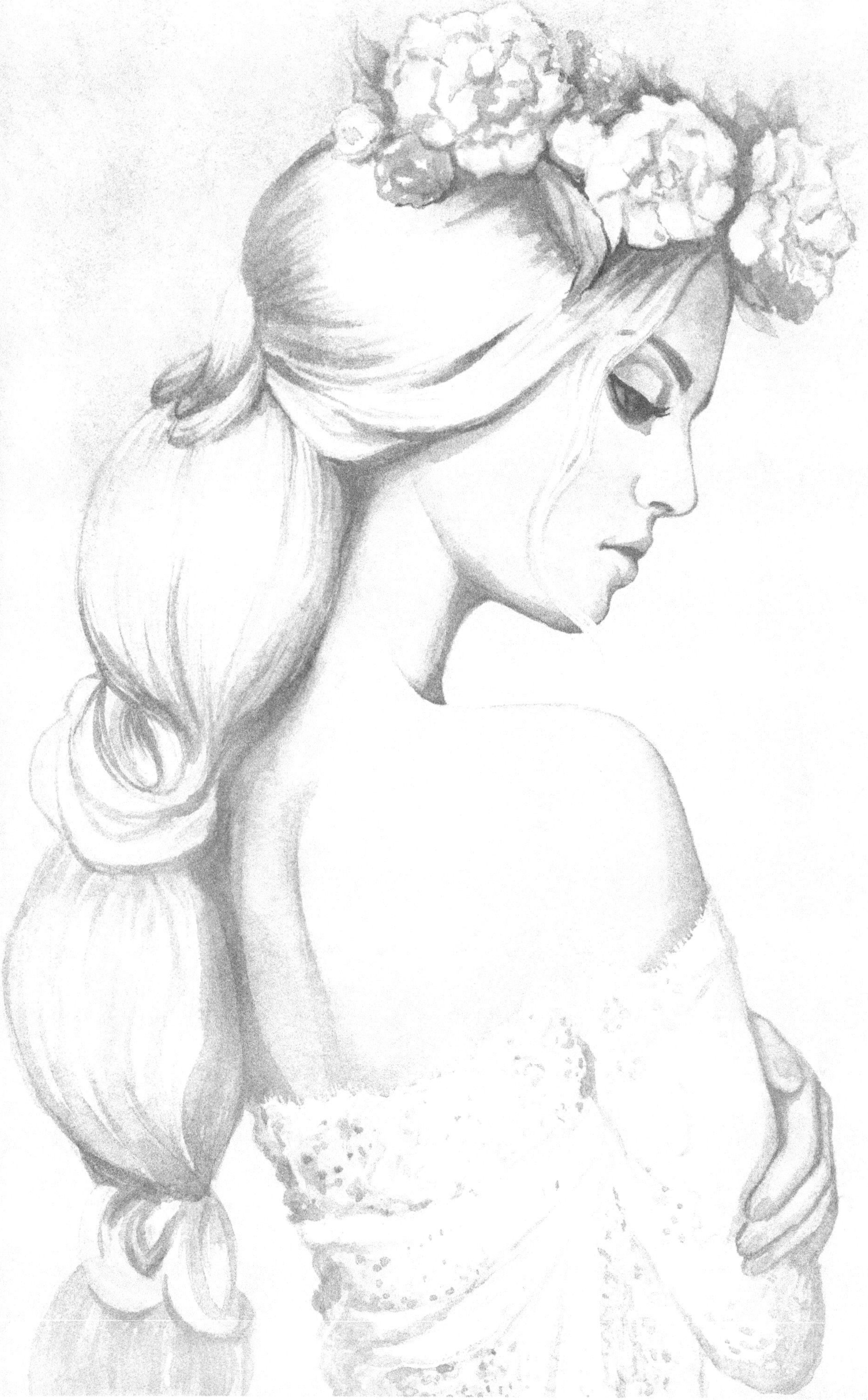

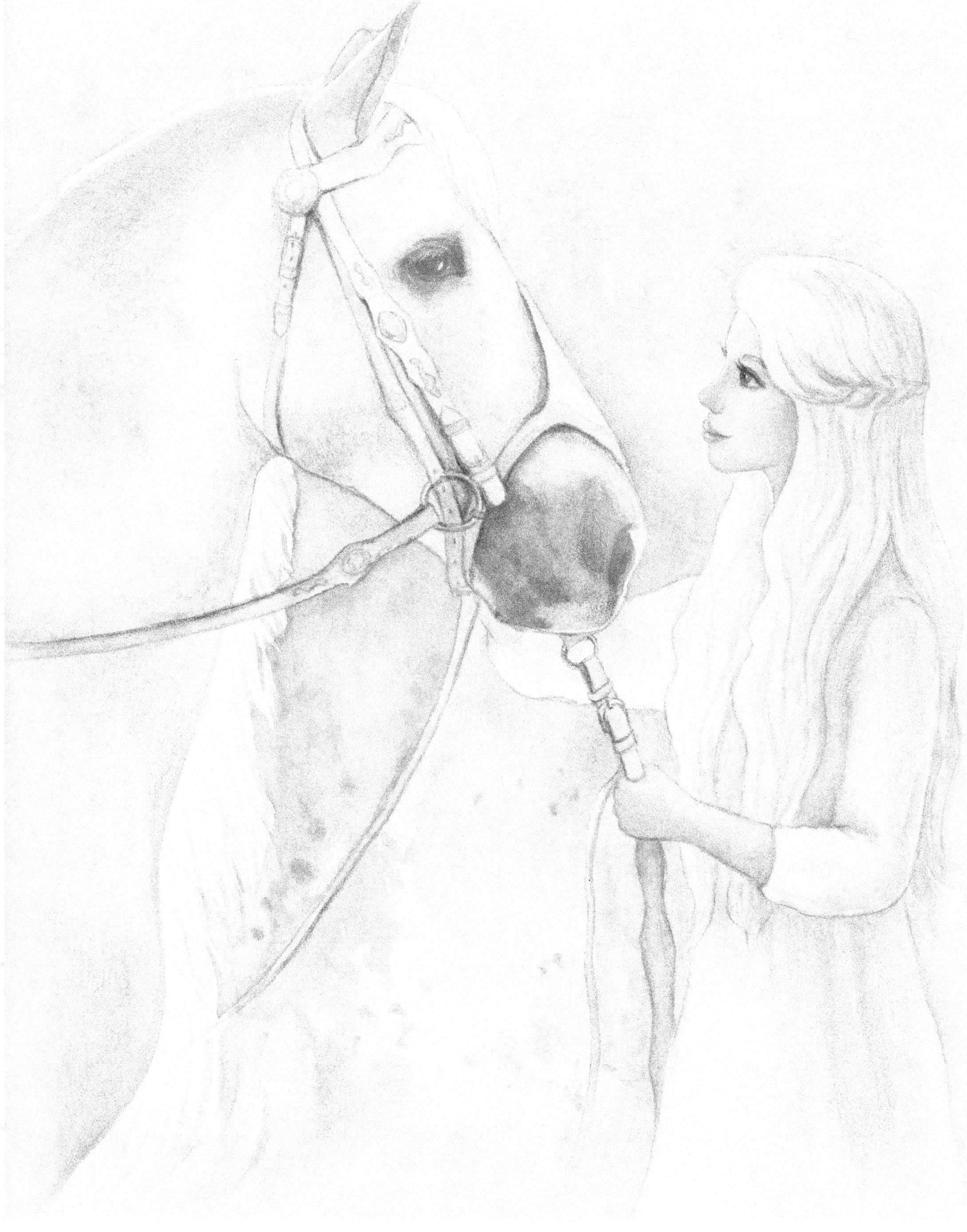

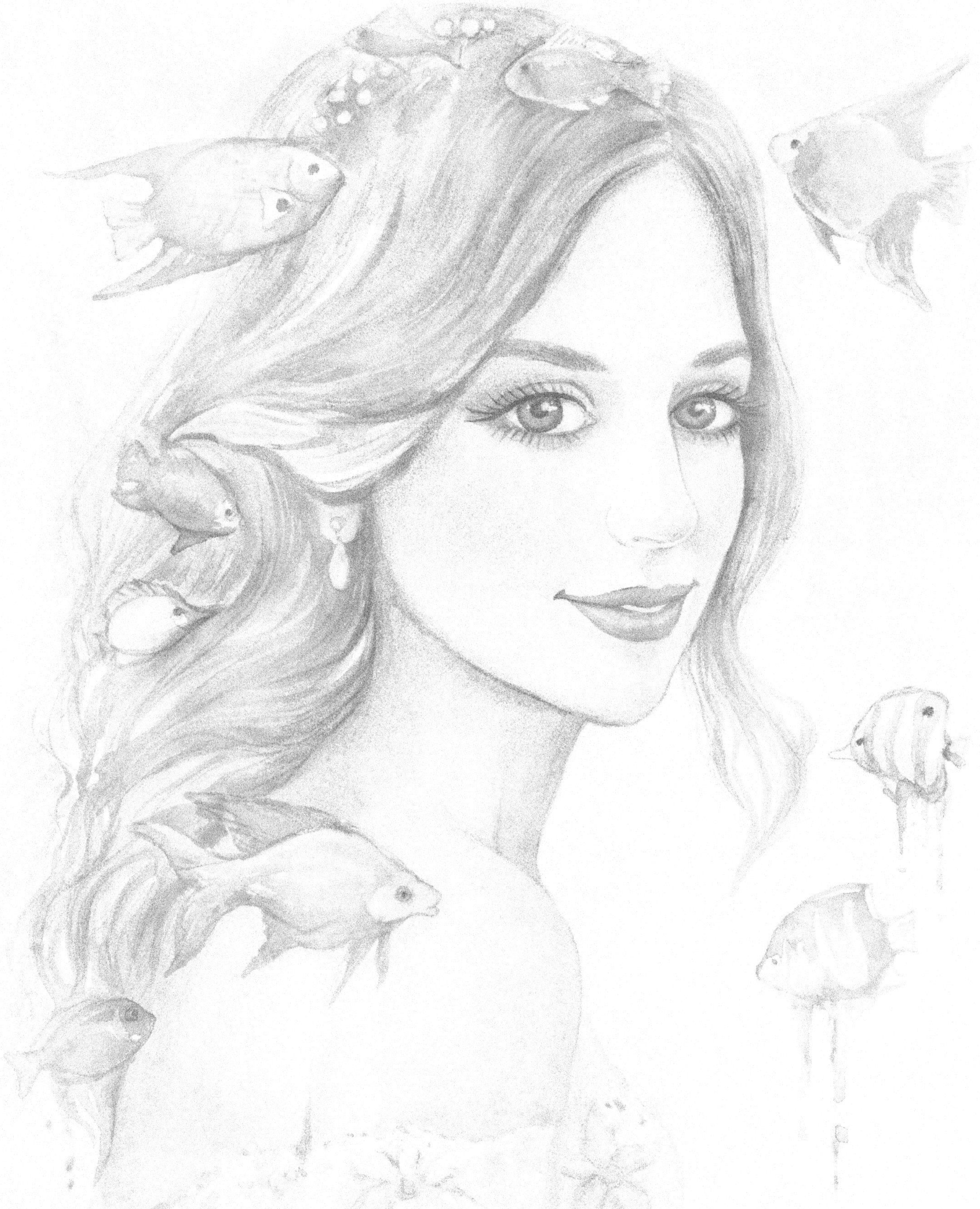

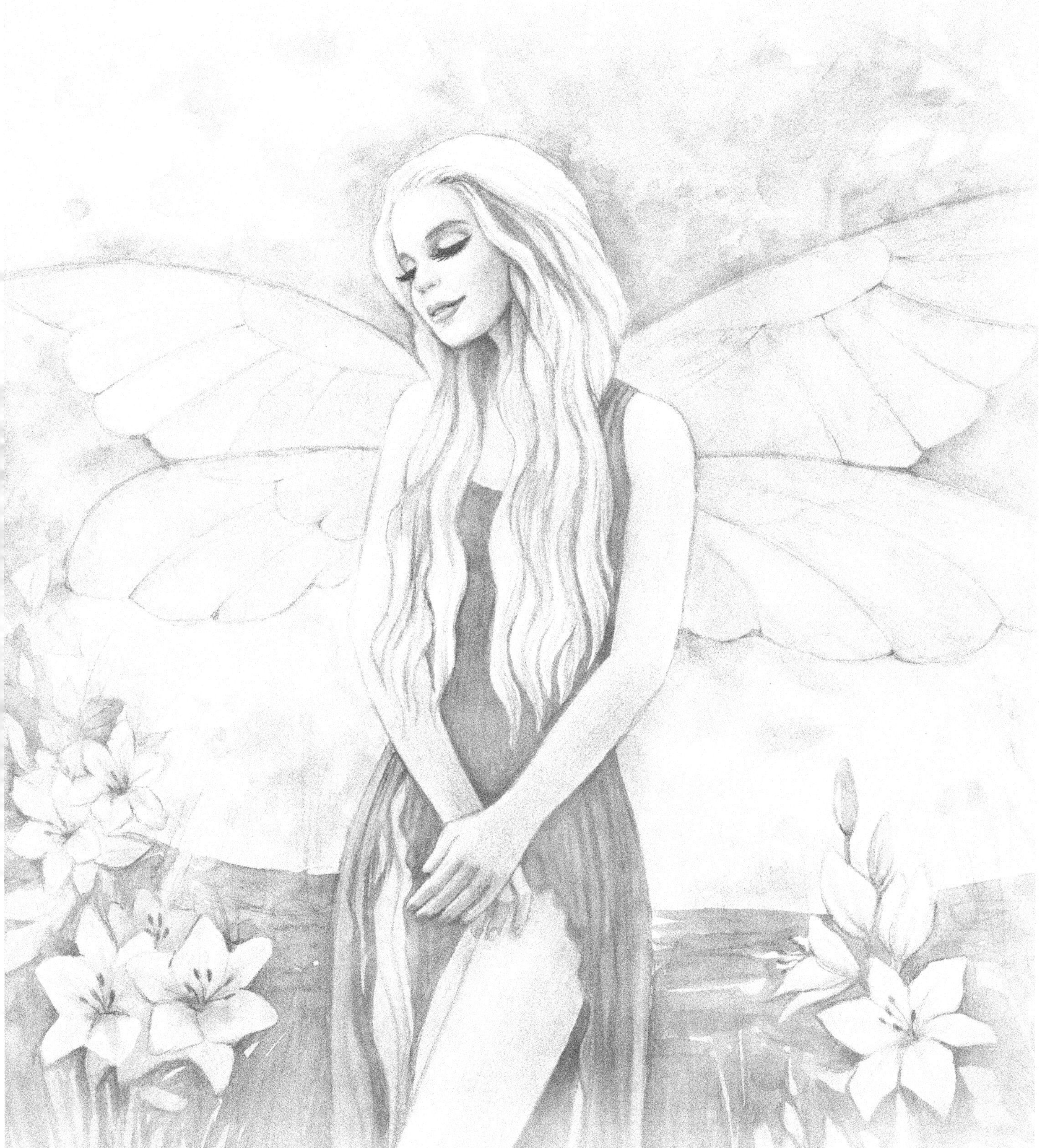

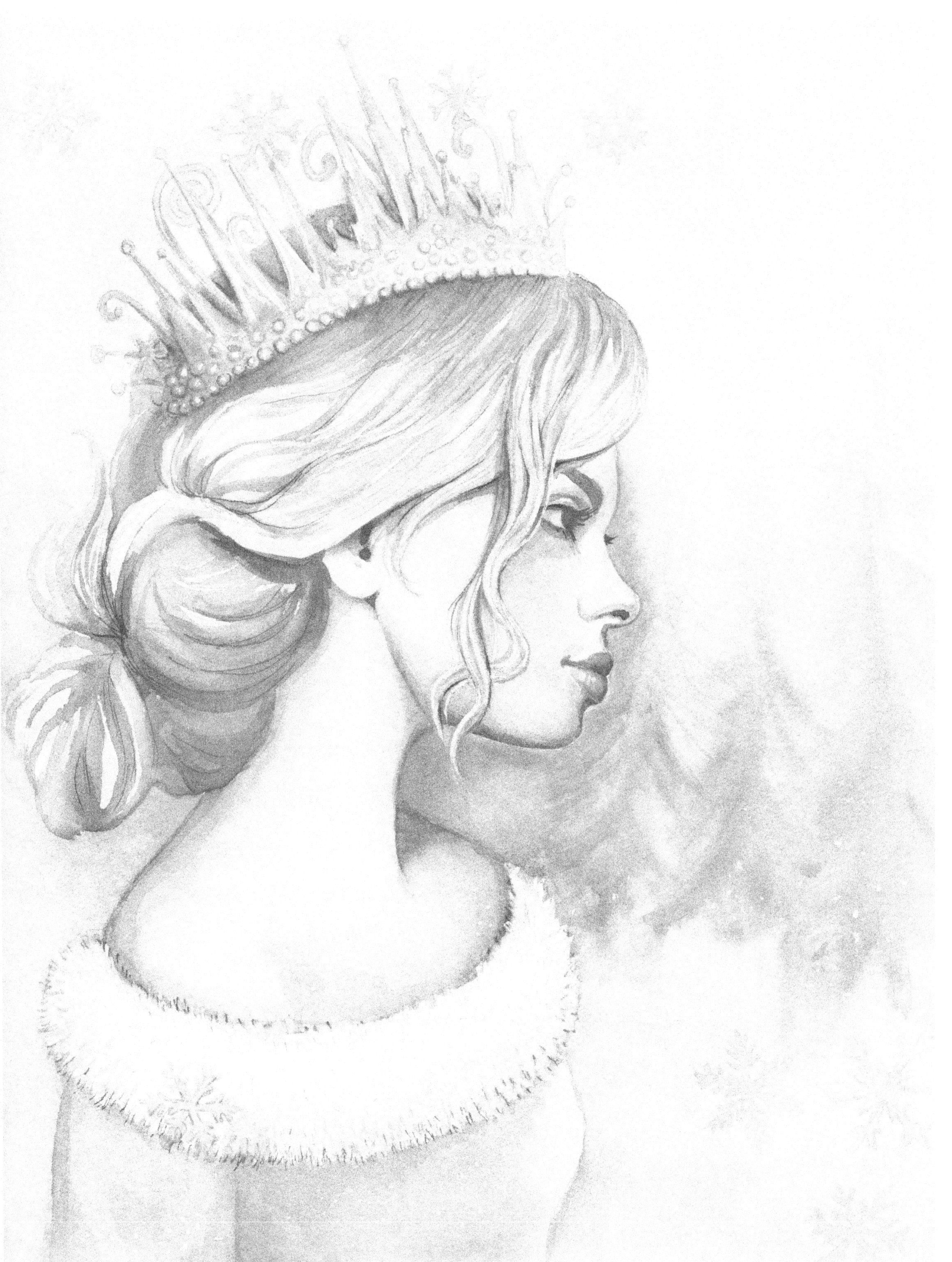

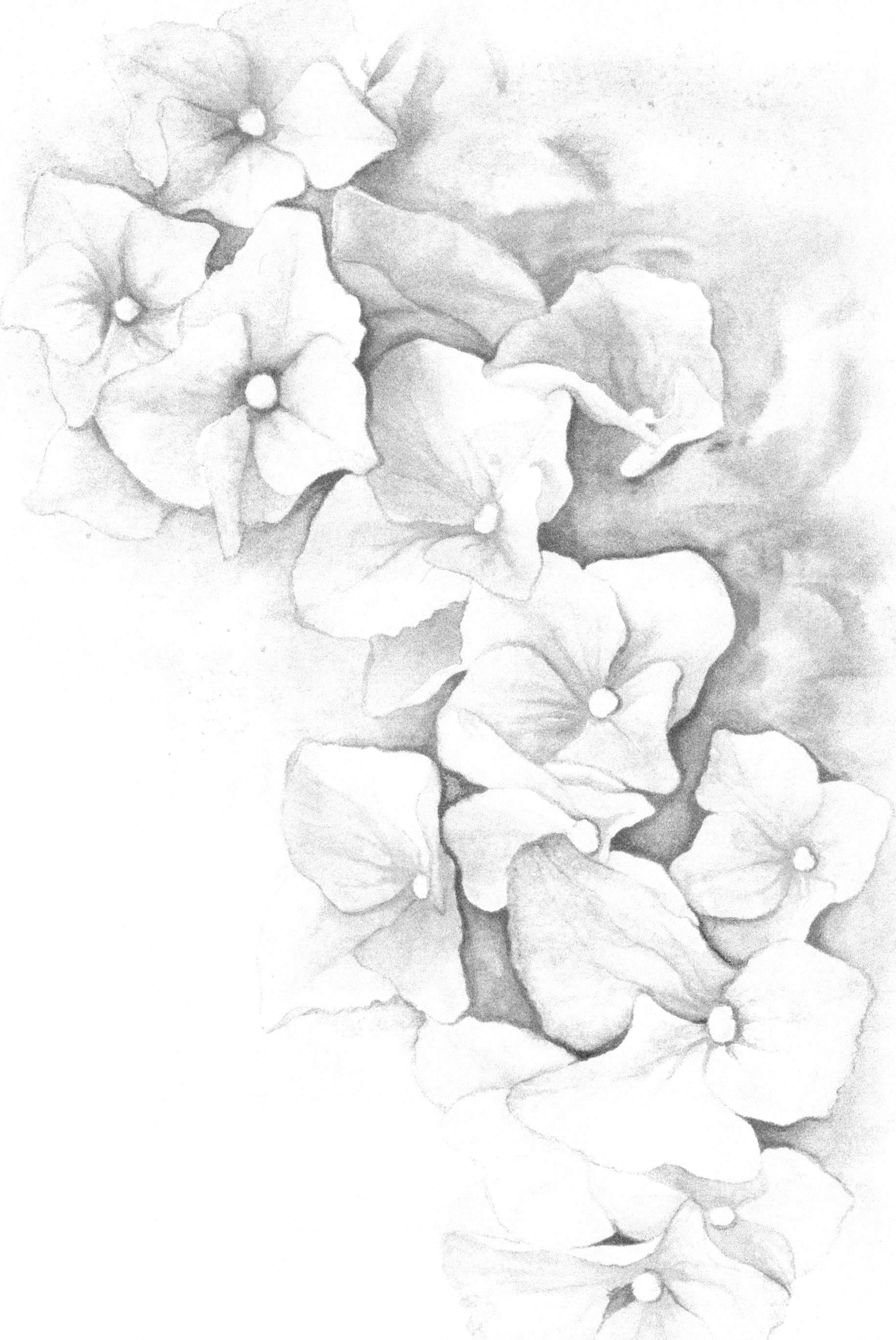

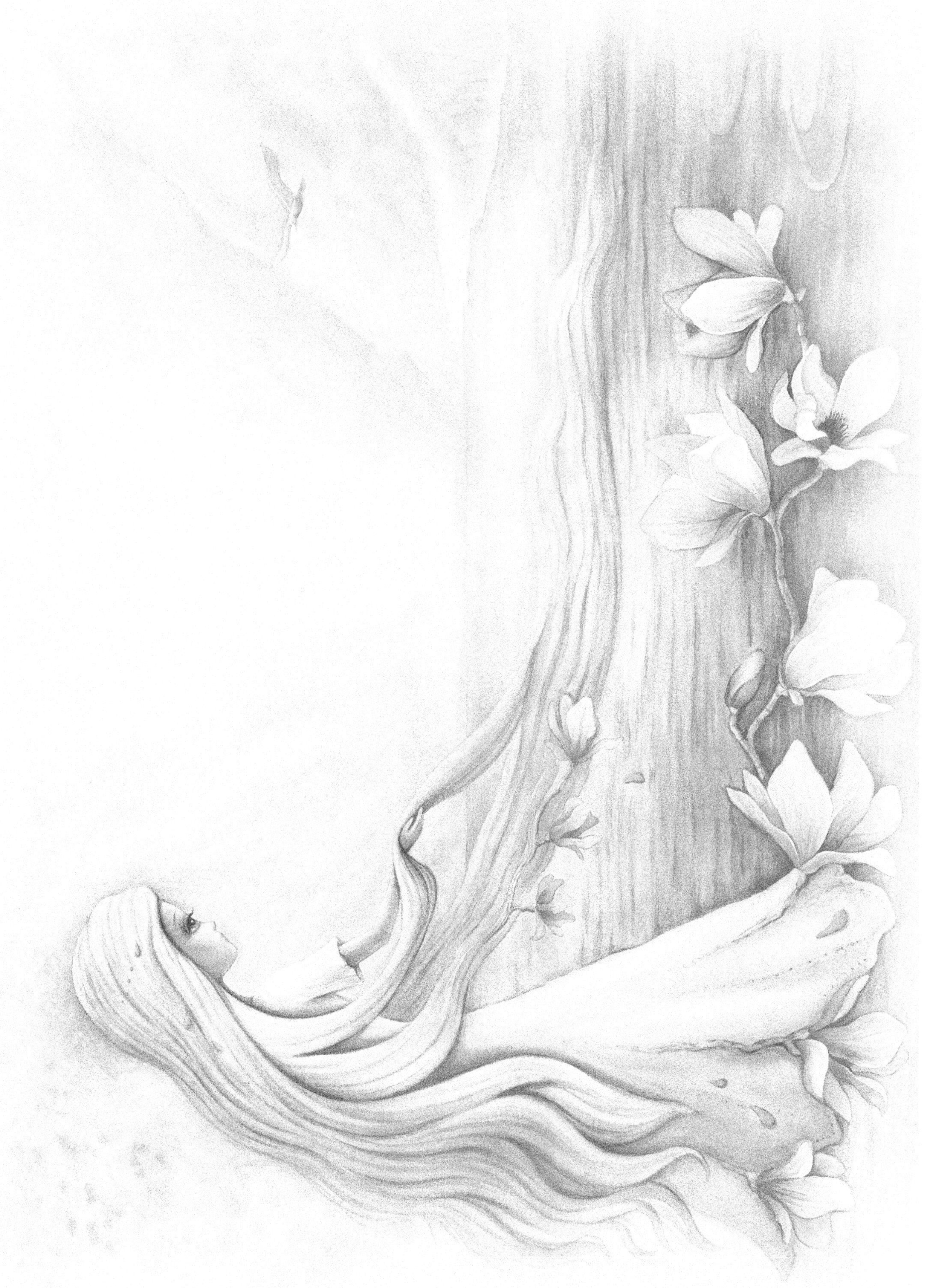

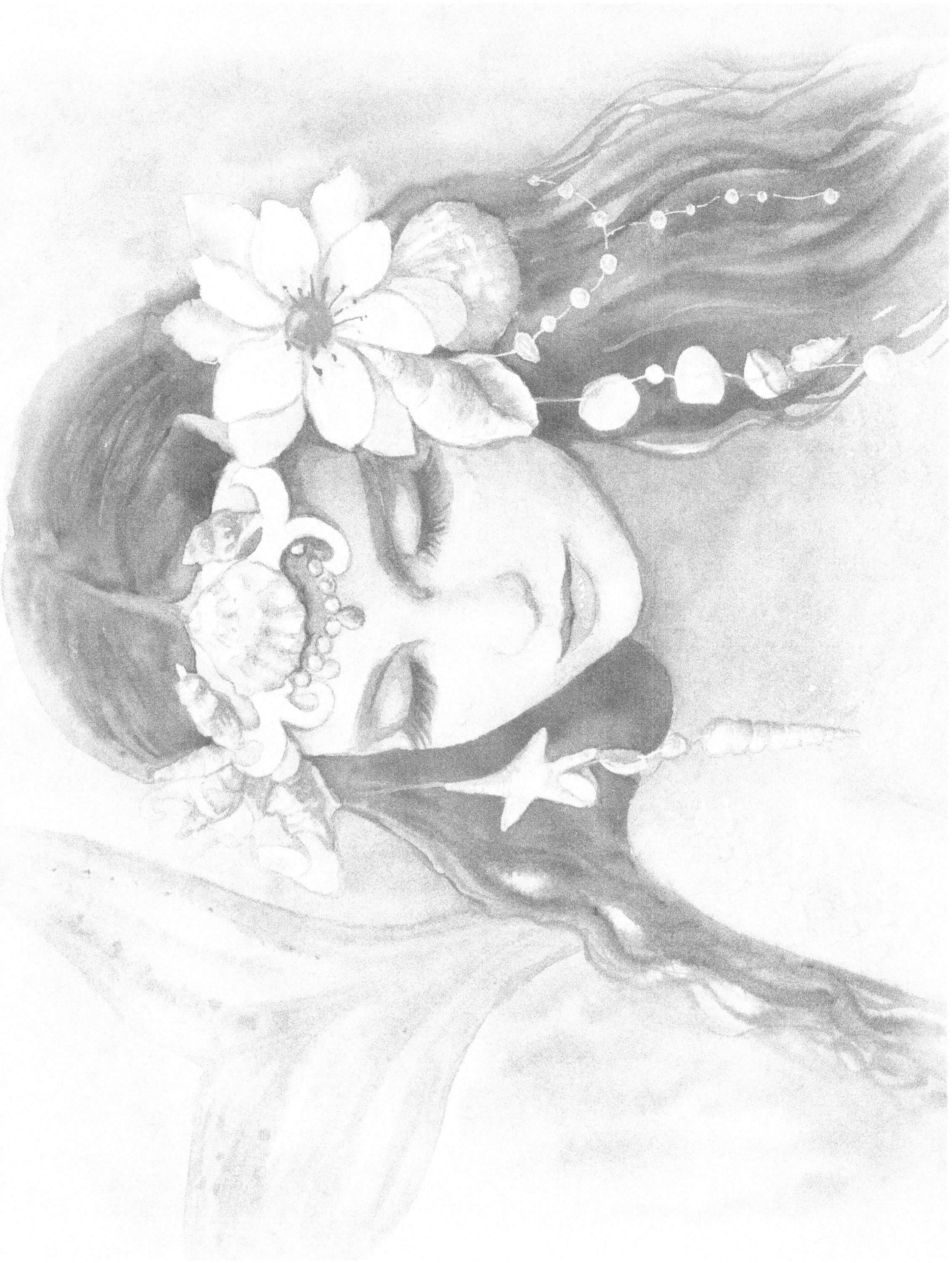

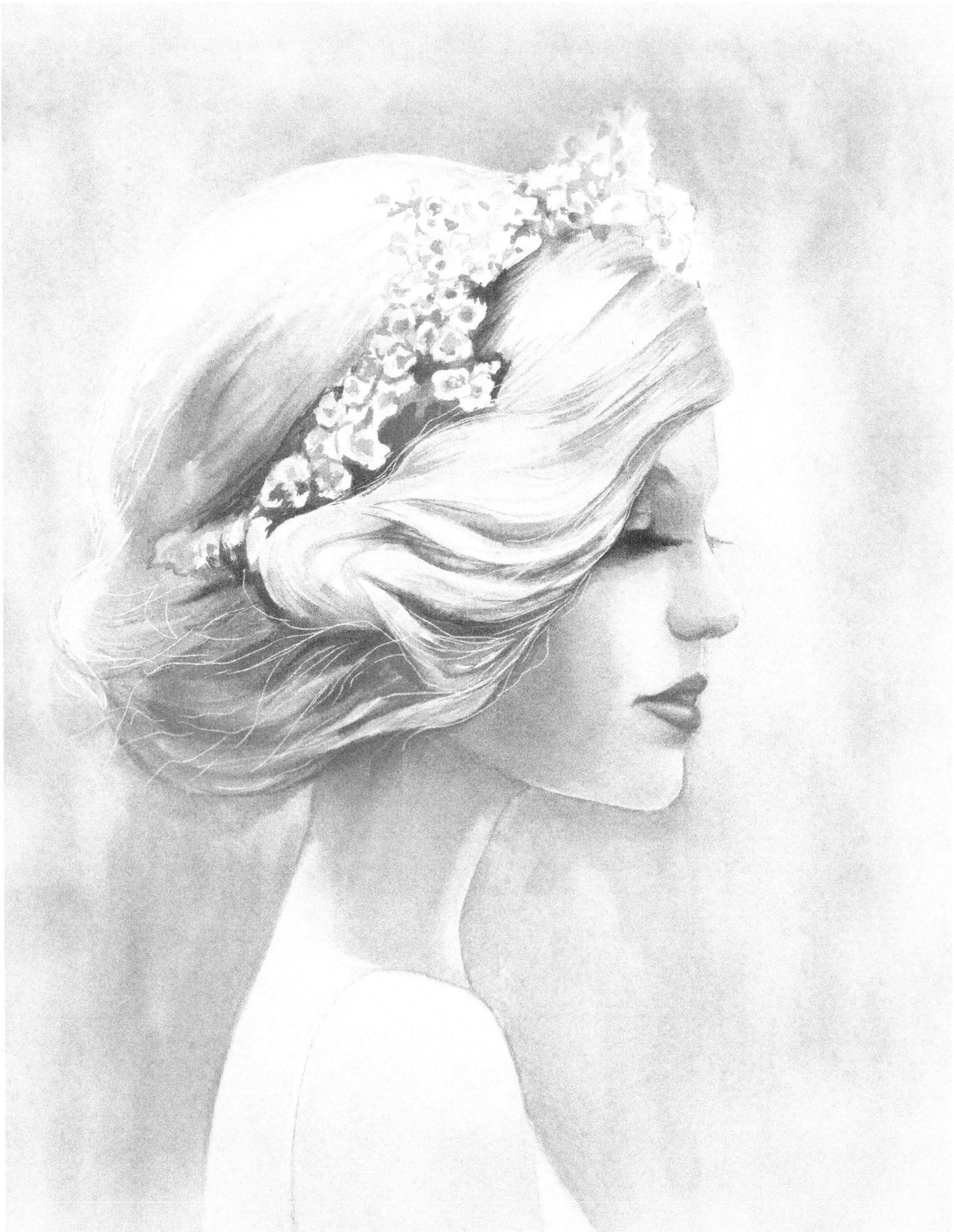

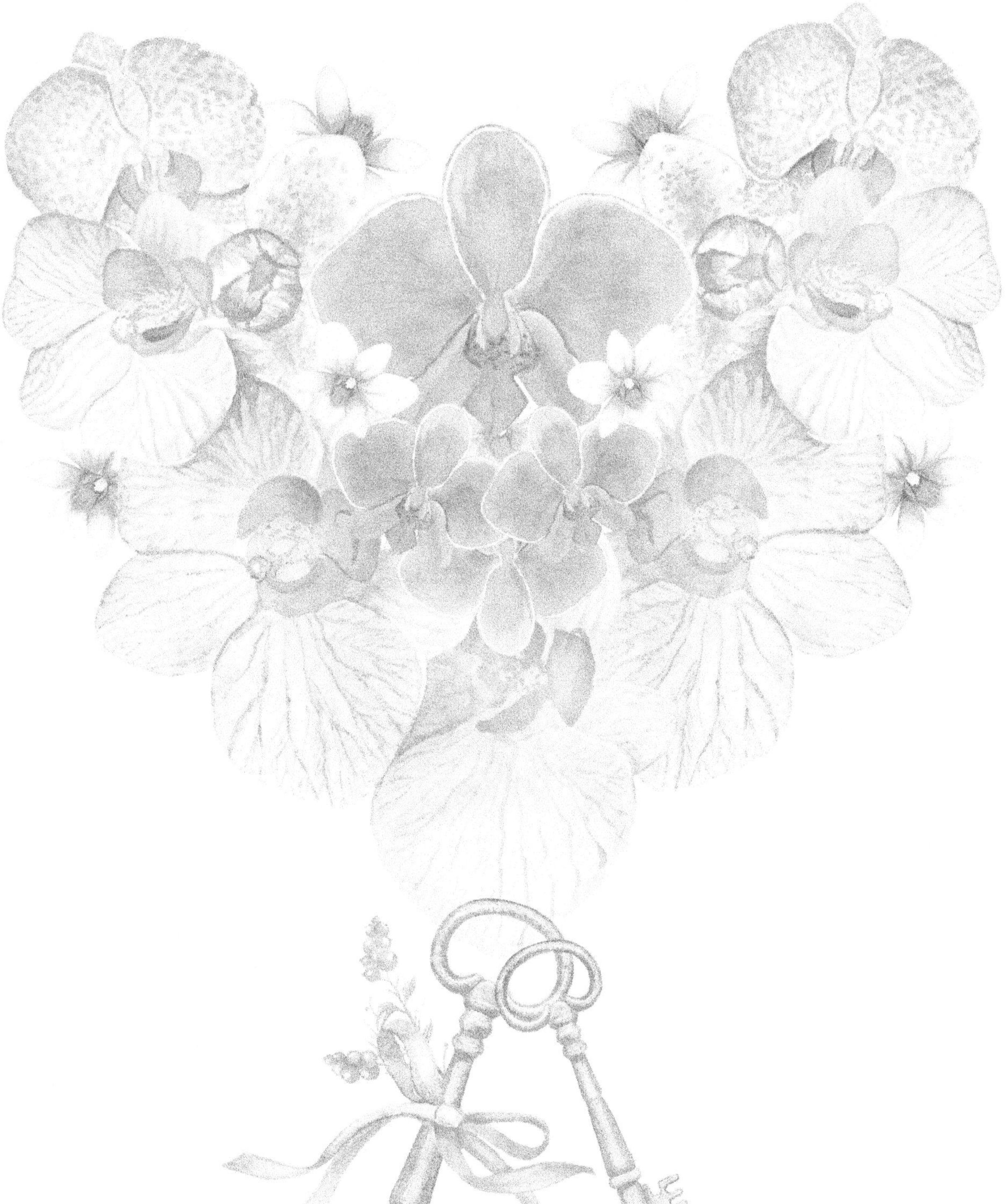

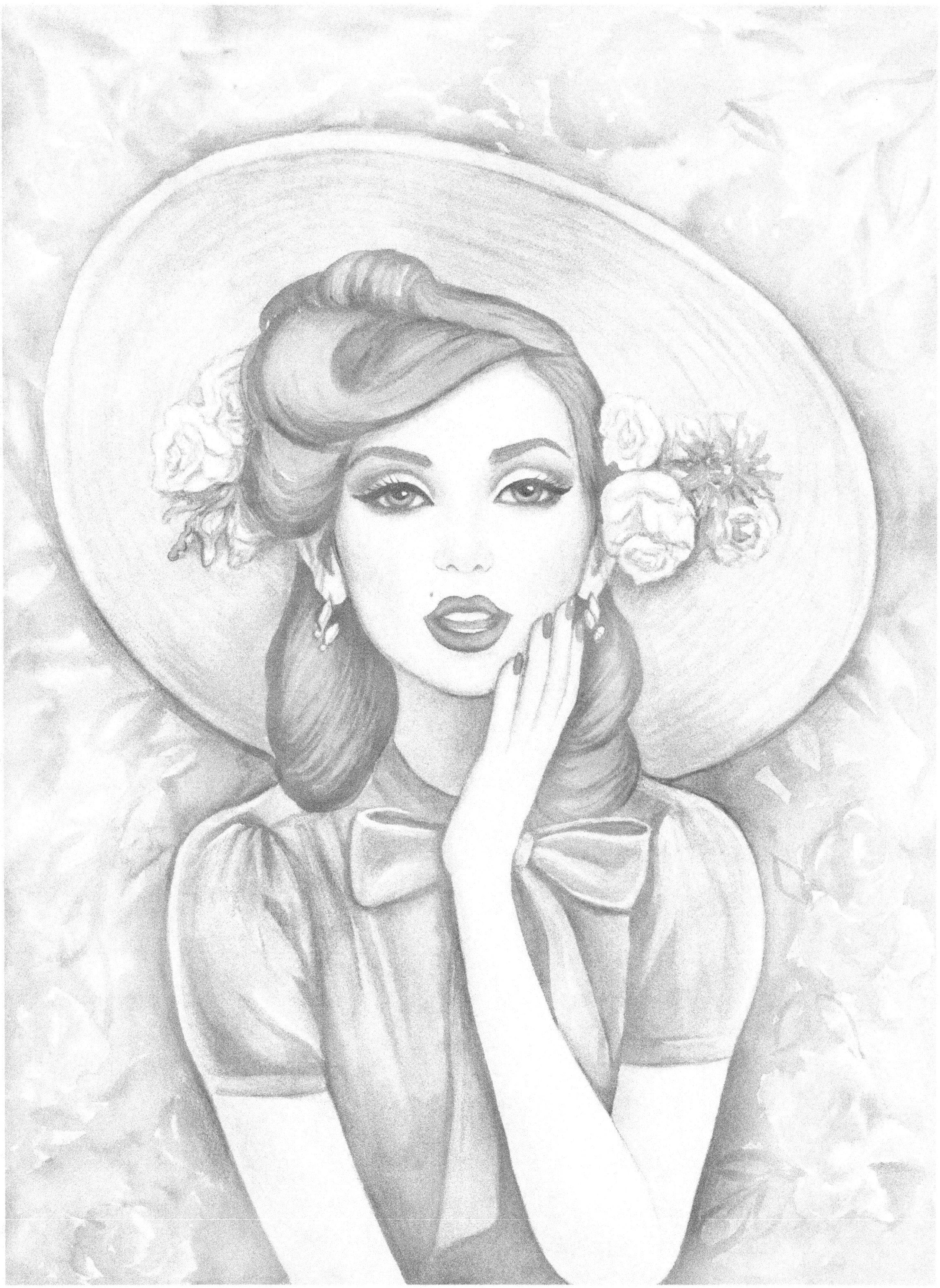

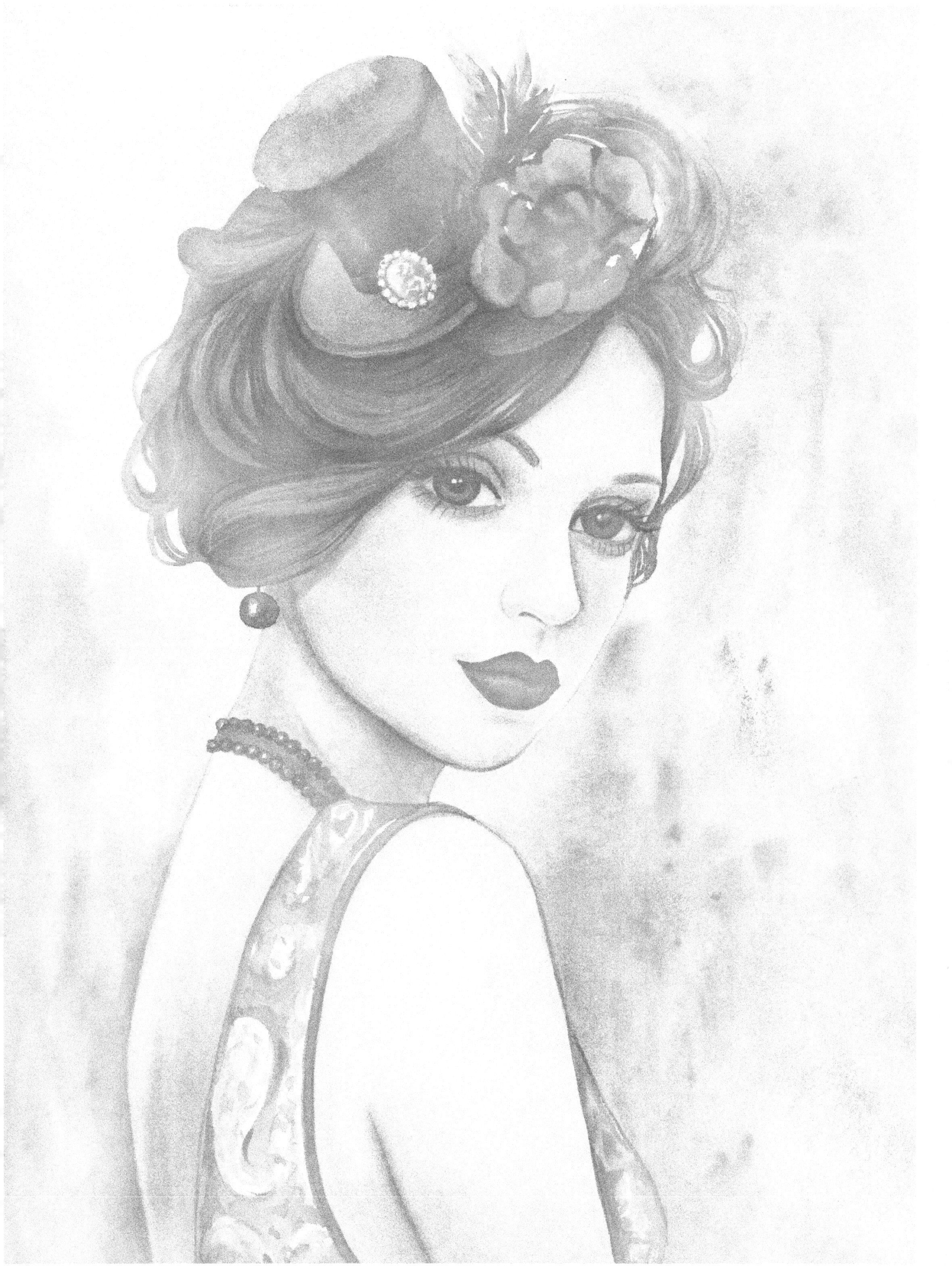

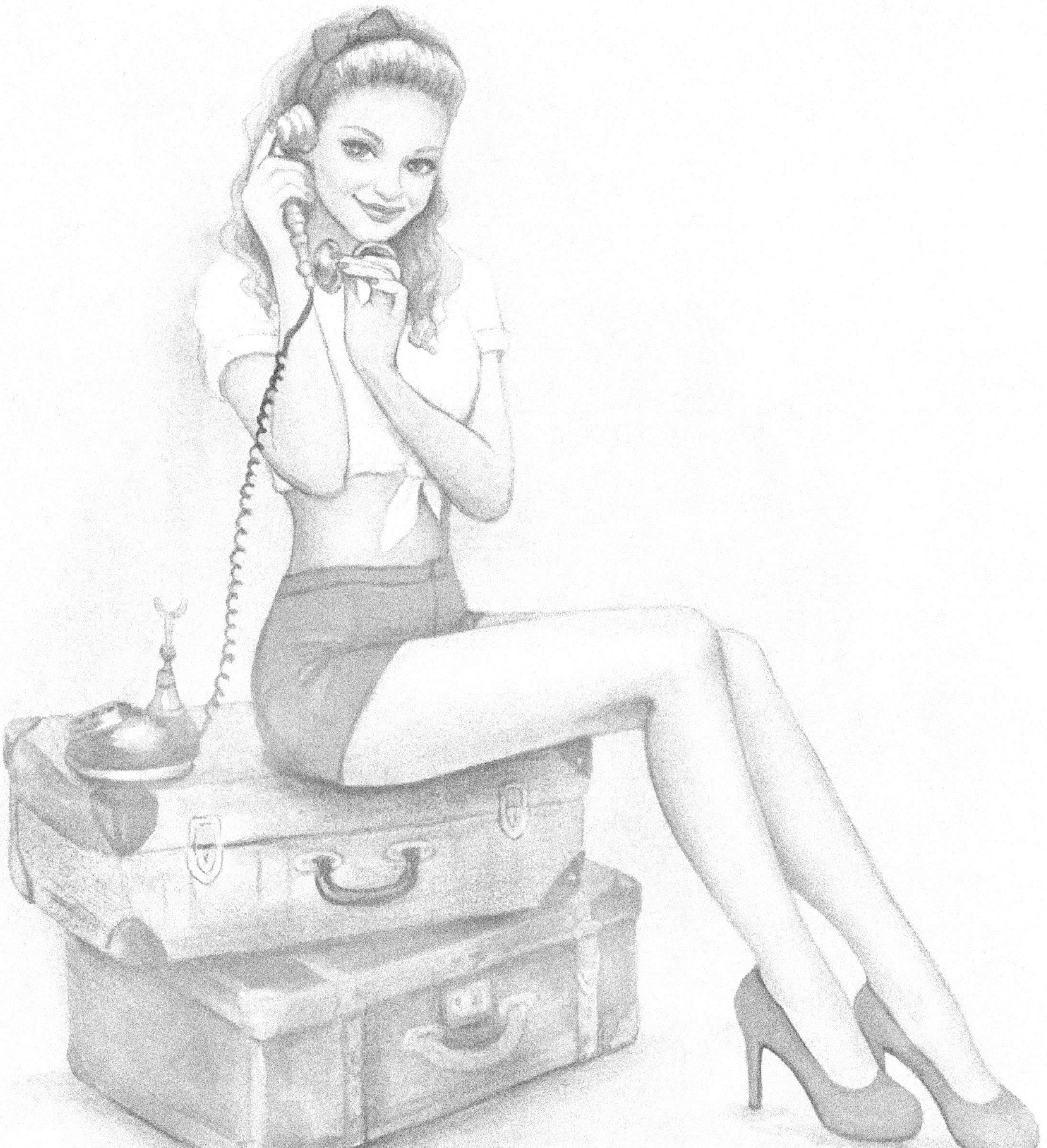

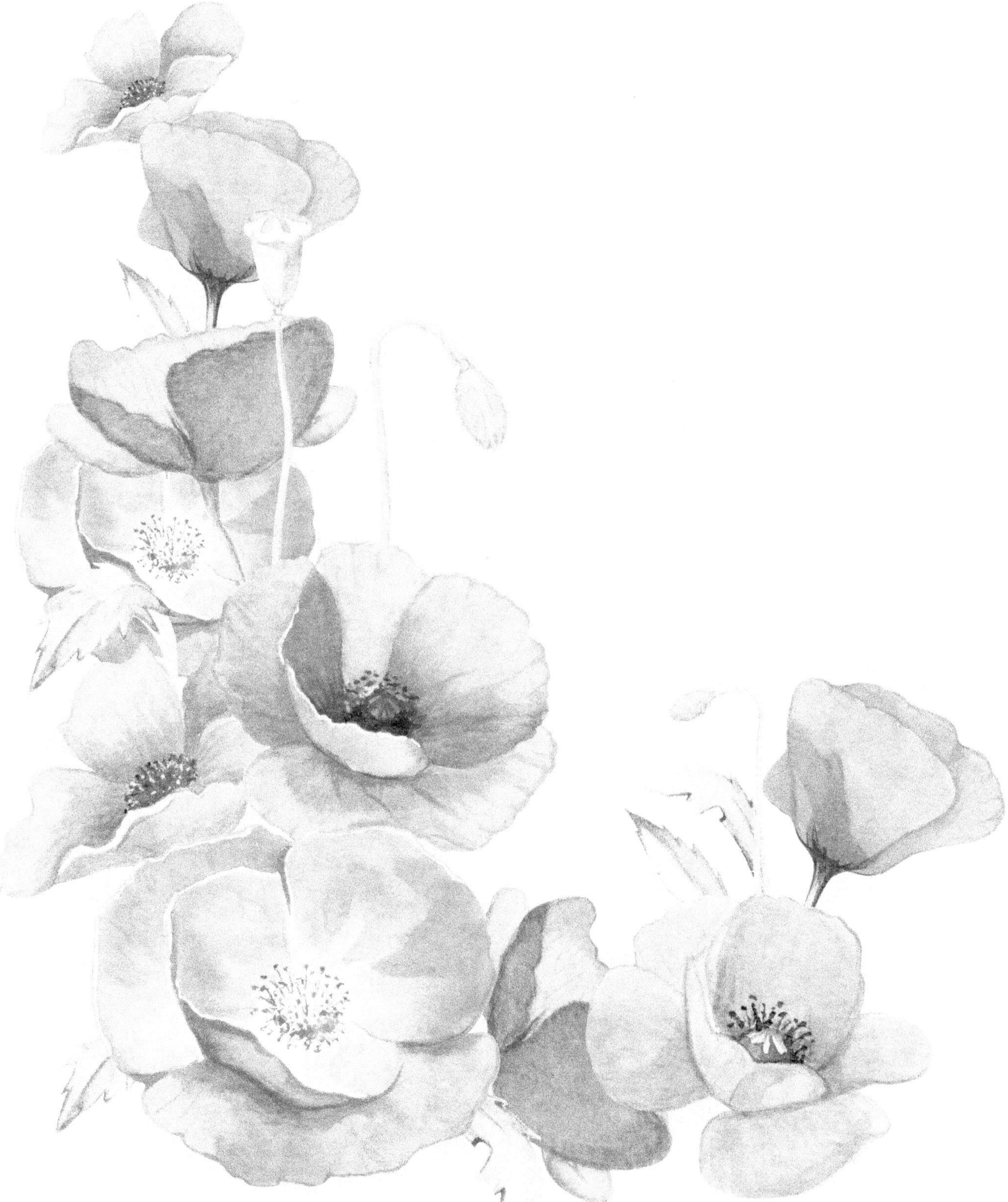

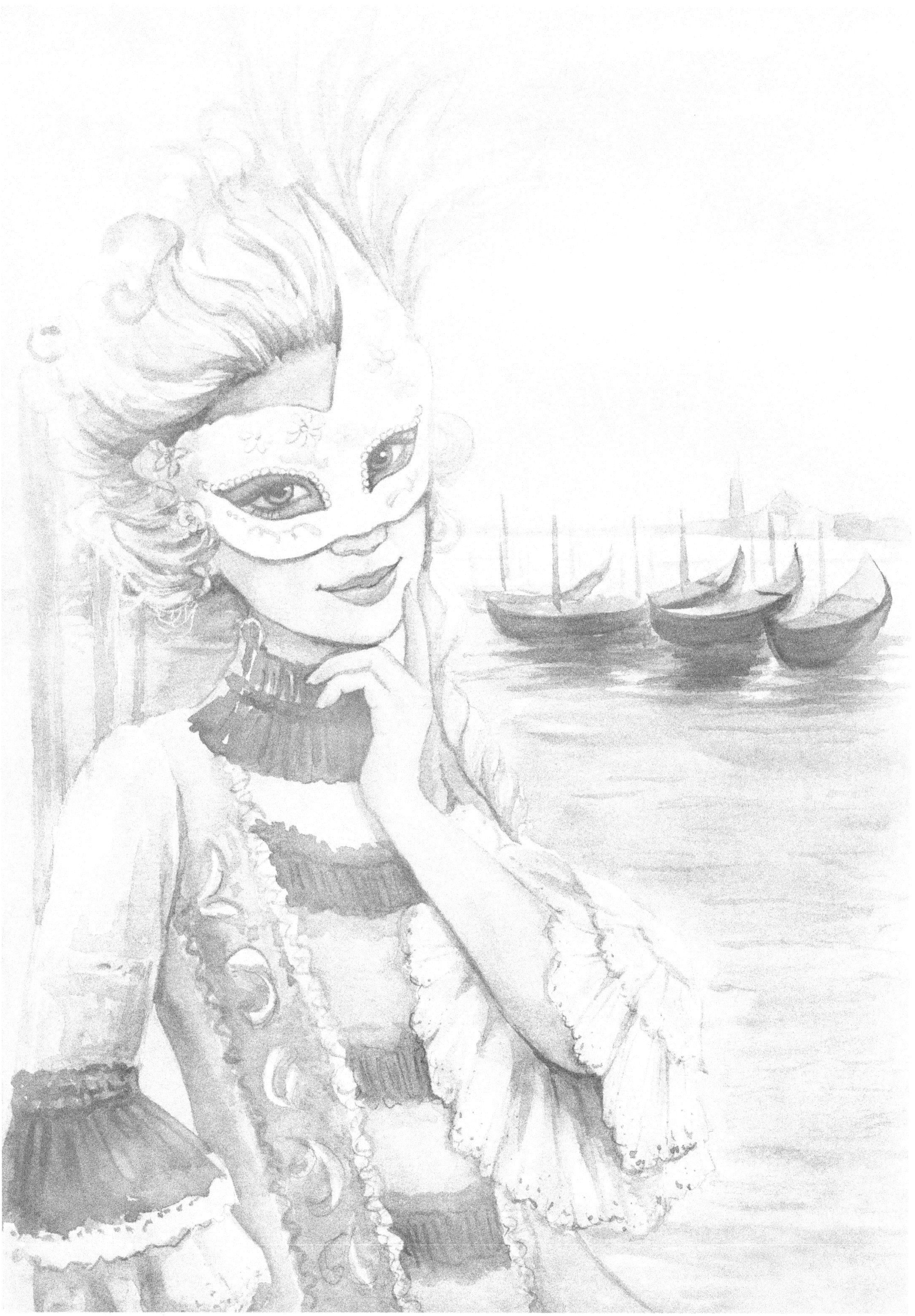

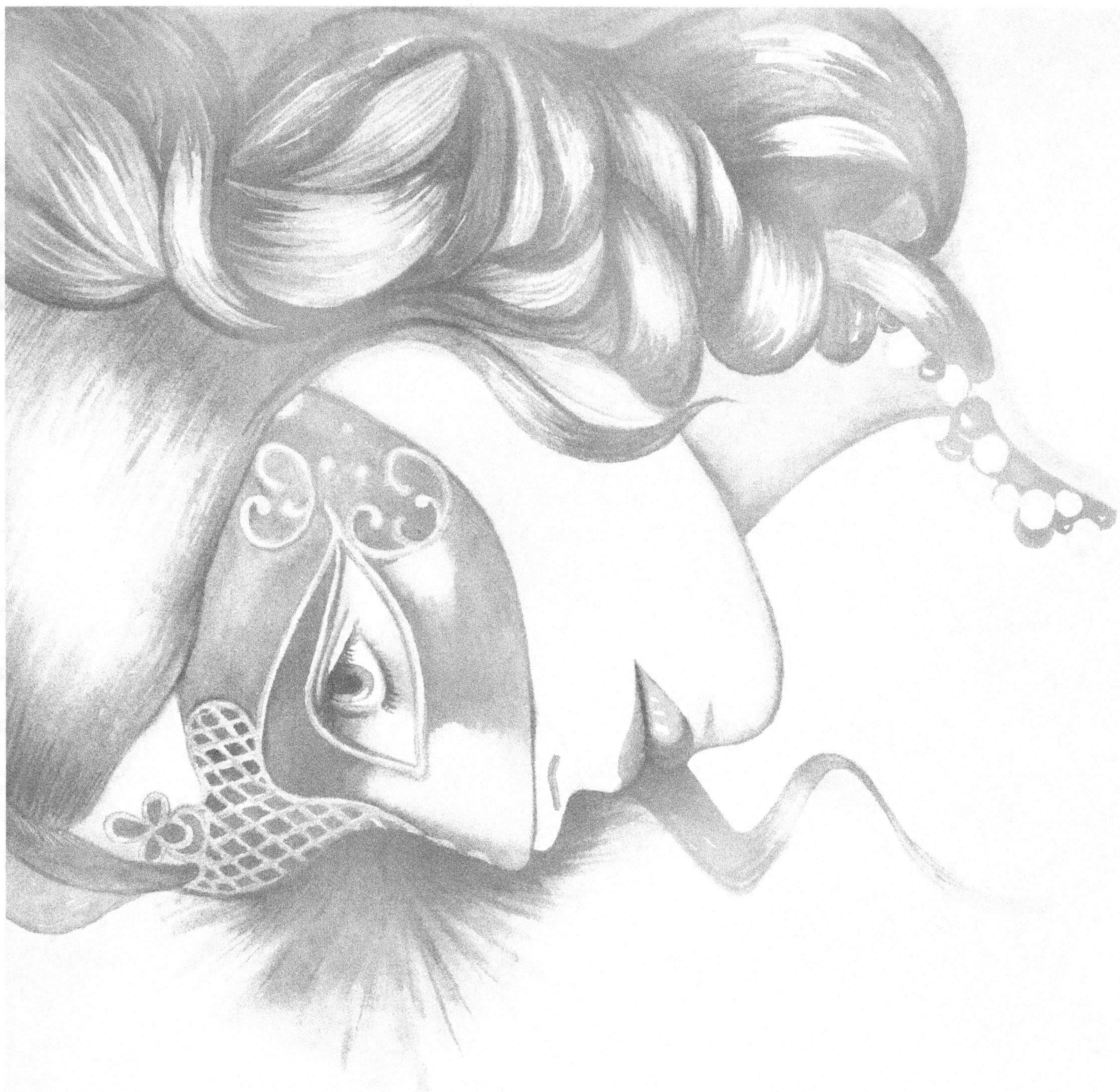

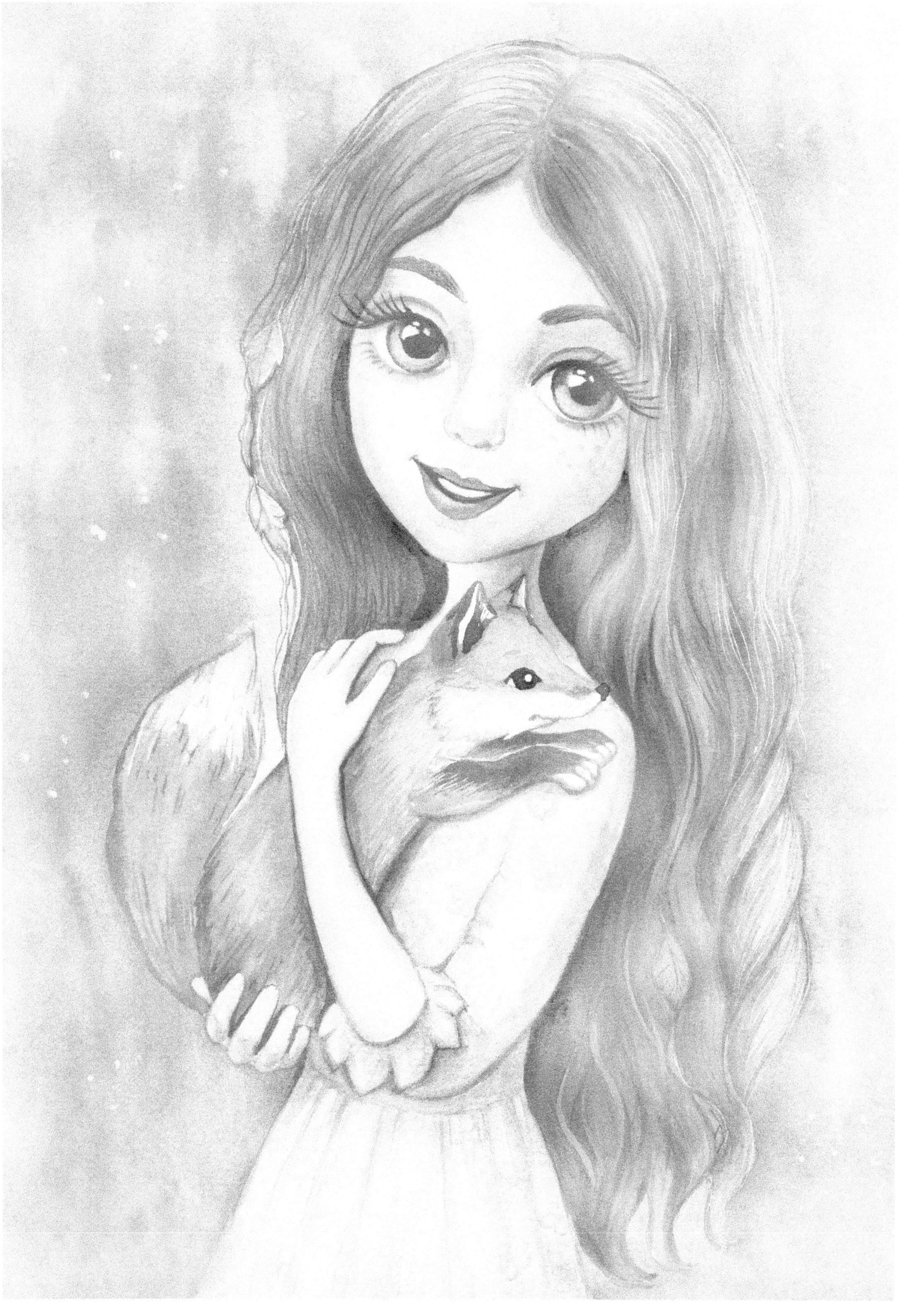

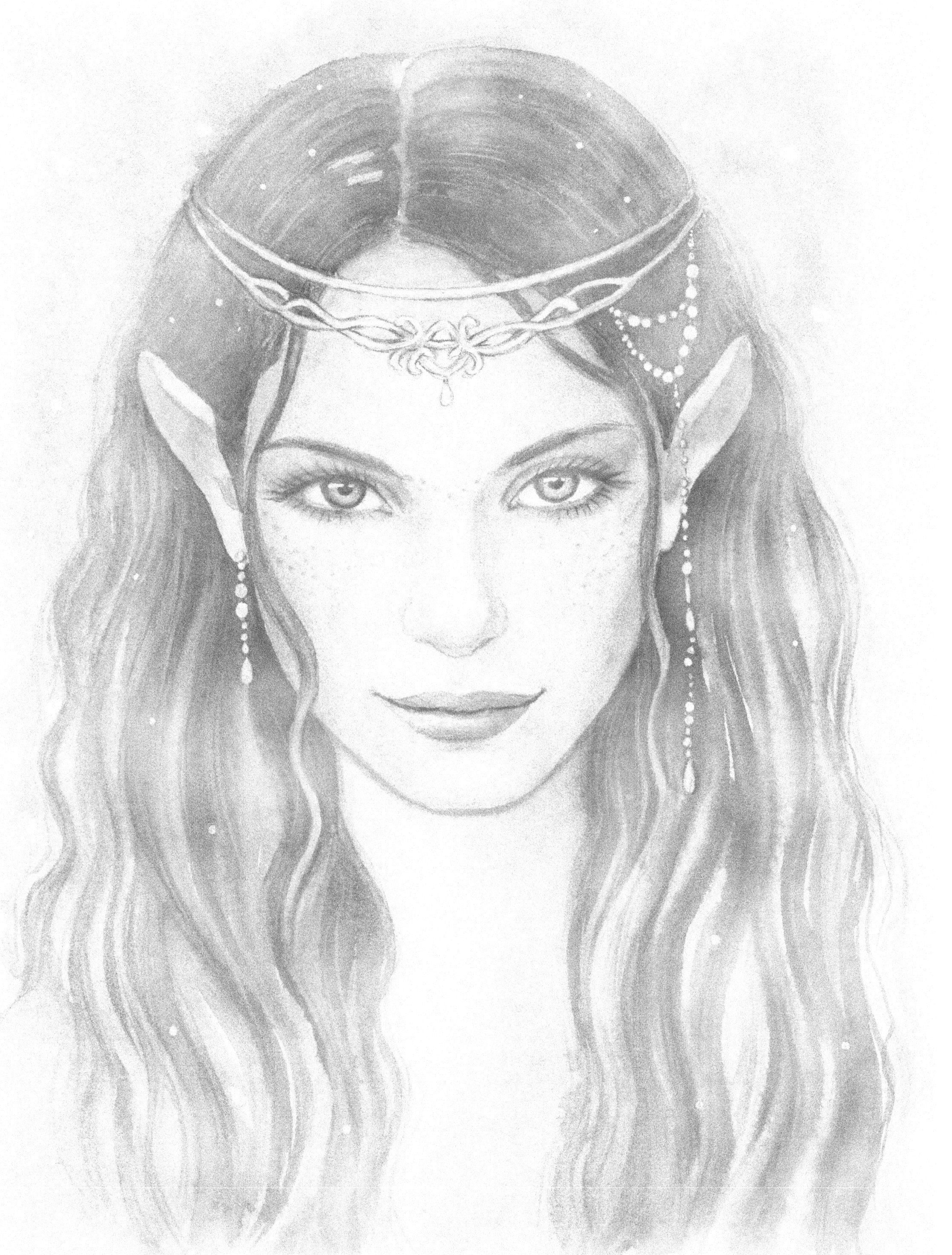

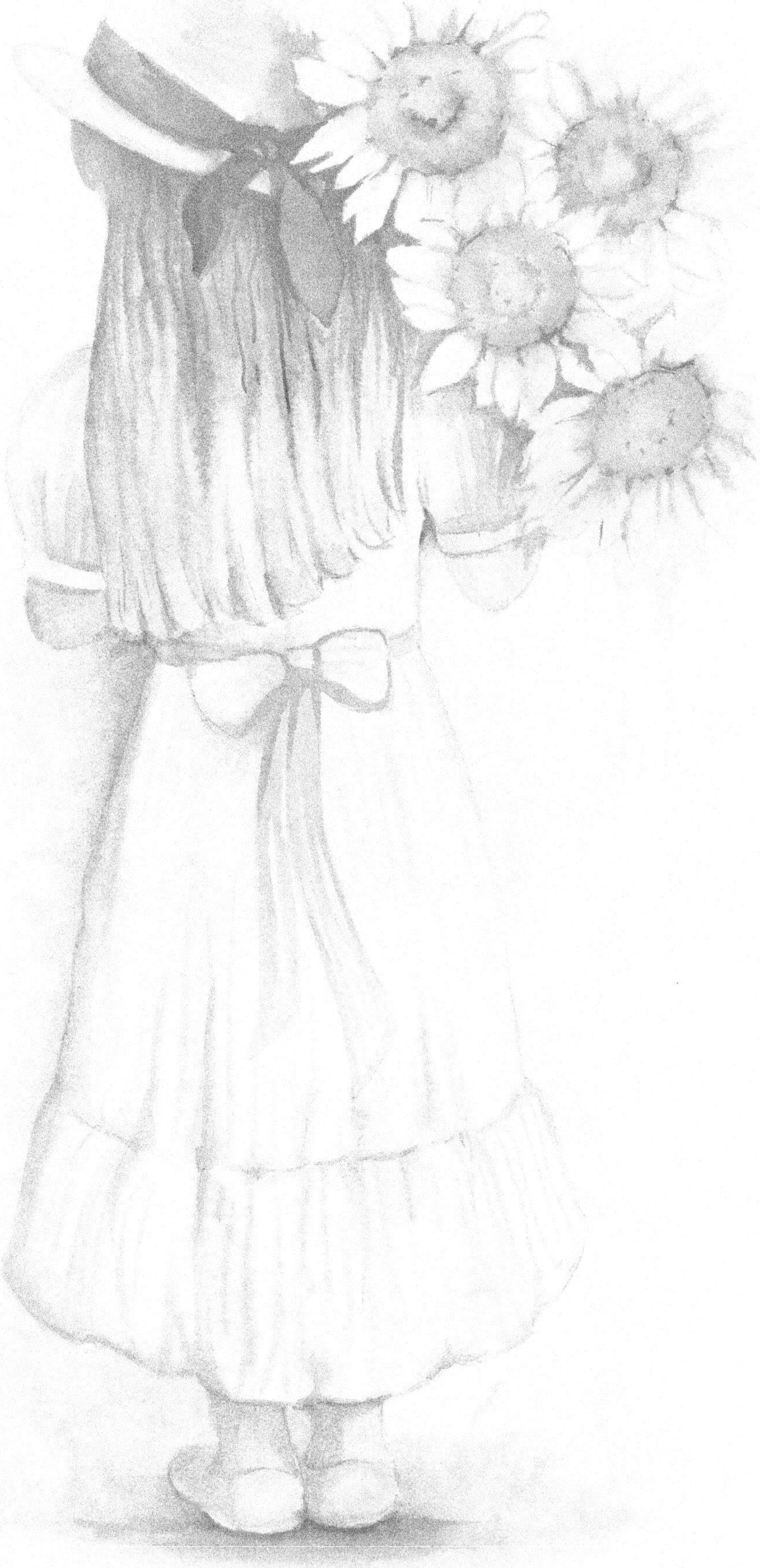

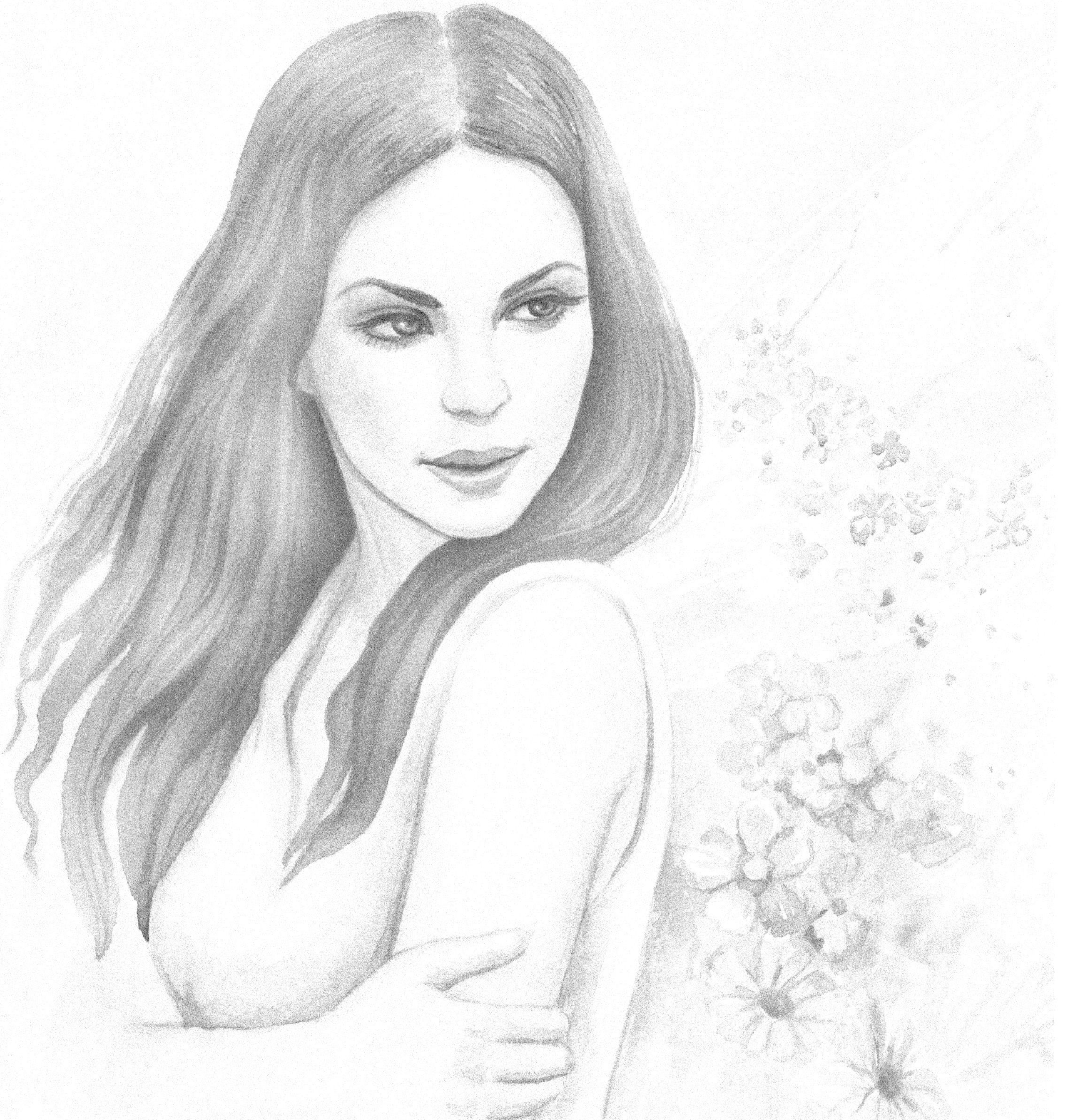

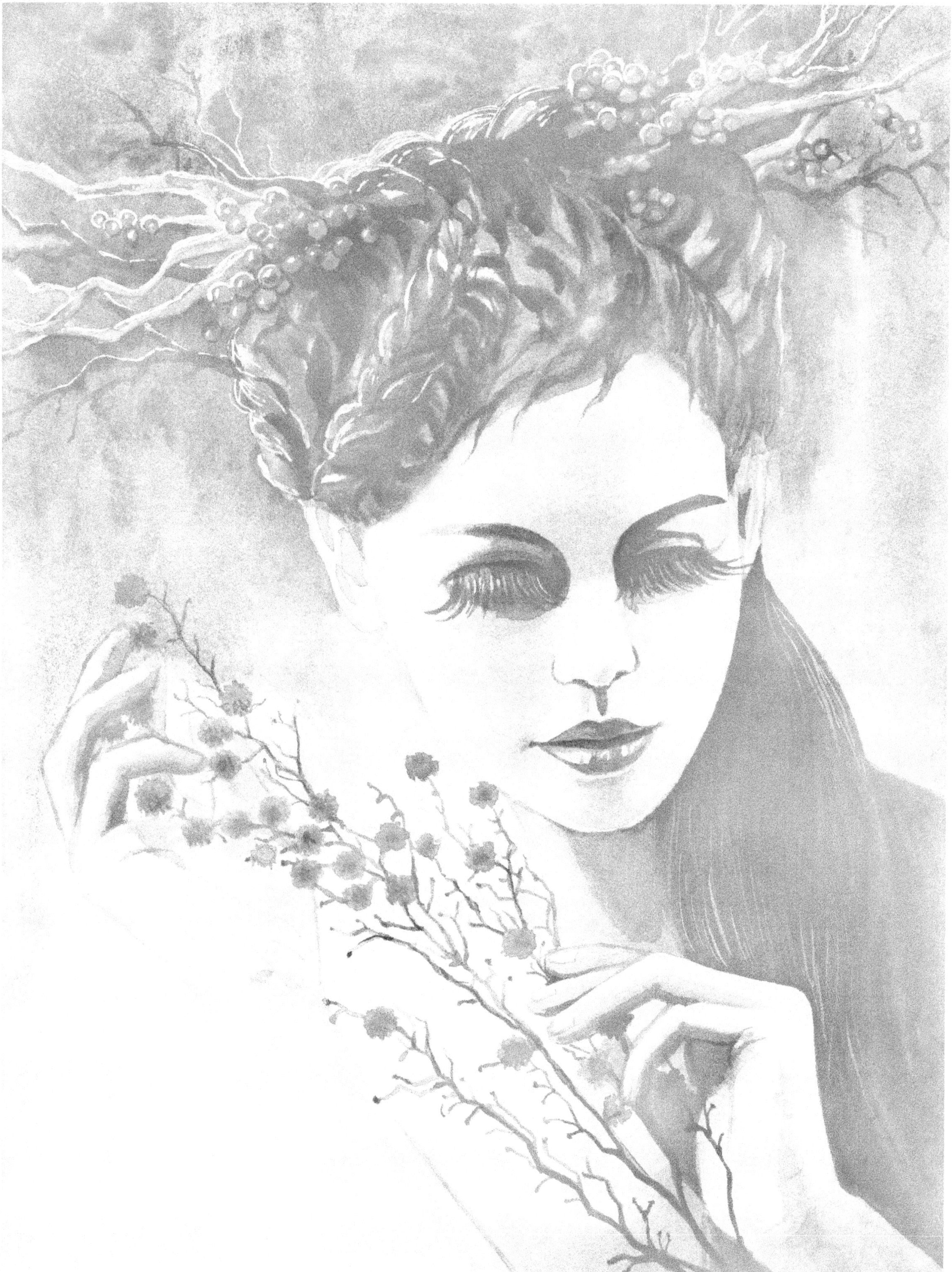

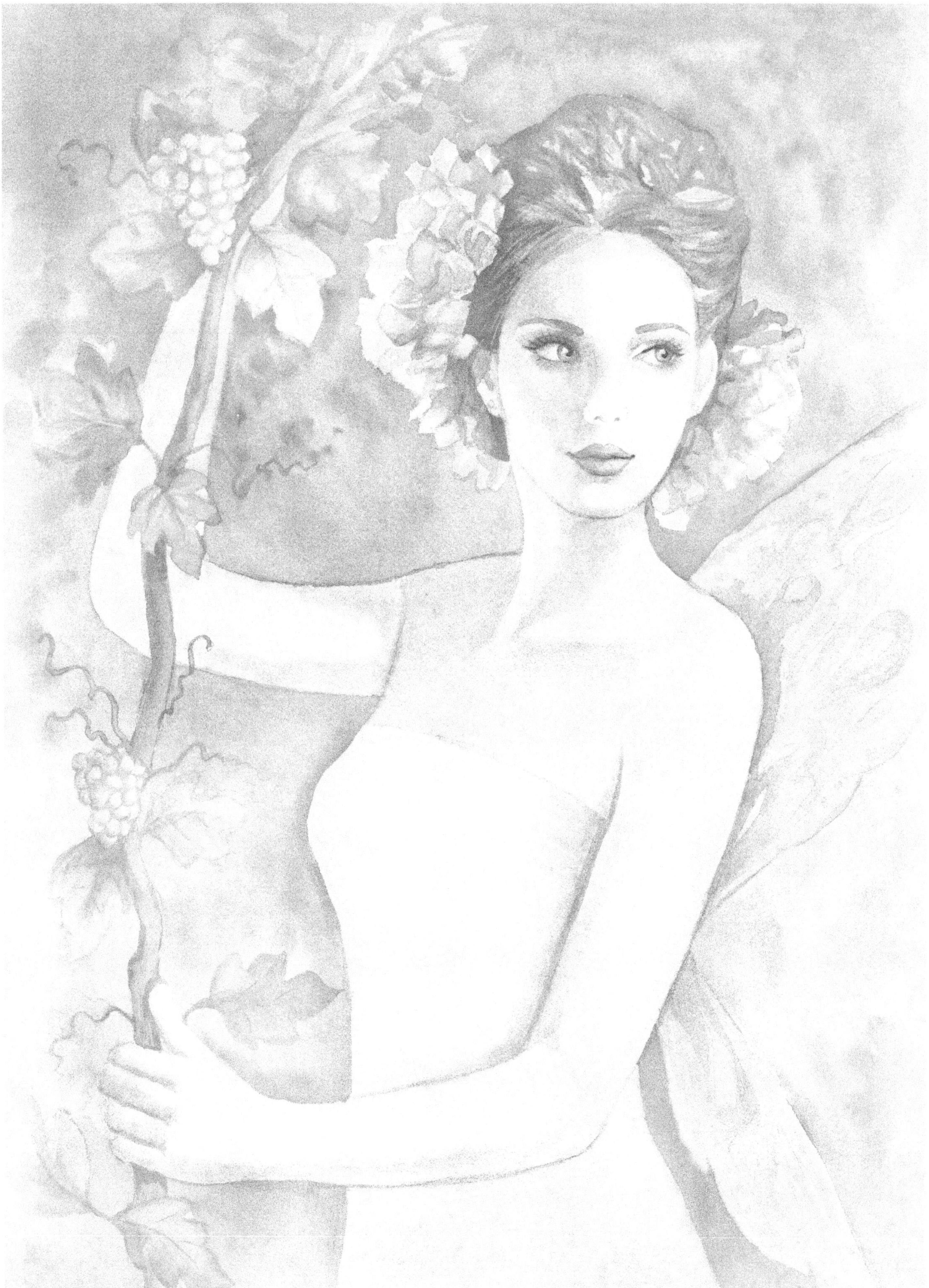

www.ingramcontent.com/pod-product-compliance
Lightning Source LLC
Chambersburg PA
CBHW082347220526
45470CB00008B/2672
* 9 7 8 8 4 0 9 2 4 7 3 9 4 *